THE CHILDREN'S BOOK OF THE FUTURE

Written by Lavie Tidhar and Richard Watson

Illustrated by Cinthya Álvarez

MARS CABBAGE

THE BEST YETI

DK

Written by Lavie Tidhar and Richard Watson
Illustrated by Cinthya Álvarez

Editor Becca Arlington
Project Art Editor Bettina Myklebust Støvne
US Senior Editor Shannon Beatty
Additional Editorial Rea Pikula
Senior Acquisitions Editor James Mitchem
Jacket and Sales Material Coordinator Elin Woosnam
Managing Art Editor Diane Peyton Jones
Production Editor Becky Fallowfield
Senior Production Controller Inderjit Bhullar
Art Director Mabel Chan
Managing Director Sarah Larter

First American Edition, 2024
Published in the United States by DK Publishing,
a division of Penguin Random House LLC
1745 Broadway, 20th Floor, New York, NY 10019

Text copyright © Lavie Tidhar and Richard Watson 2024
Illustration copyright © Cinthya Álvarez 2024
Layout and design copyright © Dorling Kindersley Limited 2024
24 25 26 27 28 10 9 8 7 6 5 4 3 2 1
001–338350–Jun/2024

A catalog record for this book
is available from the Library of Congress.
ISBN 978-0-7440-9802-0

DK books are available at special discounts
when purchased in bulk for sales promotions,
premiums, fund-raising, or educational use.
For details, contact: DK Publishing Special Markets,
1745 Broadway, 20th Floor, New York, NY 10019
SpecialSales@dk.com

Printed and bound in China

www.dk.com

MIX
Paper | Supporting
responsible forestry
FSC™ C018179

This book was made with Forest
Stewardship Council™ certified
paper – one small step in DK's
commitment to a sustainable future.
Learn more at
www.dk.com/uk/information/sustainability

CONTENTS

Part 1: Earth

Part 2: Life on land and sea

PREFACE

As writers, we think about the future a lot. We imagine dozens of different futures, often before breakfast! Some of these futures are good, some are bad, and some are just really weird. All are different in some way from today. They are all stories that we tell ourselves to help us think and to help others think too.

The future is where you are going to spend the rest of your life. It is up to you to shape it, to choose what kind of a future it will be. In this book, we have tried to imagine the best kinds of futures. None of them are real—at least, not yet. They start on our own, near-future Earth, and gradually grow more distant. Will we go farther into space? Should we? And what will we find there? The universe is huge, and our planet is tiny—a precious blue marble. There are billions of galaxies, stars, and planets out there. Will we meet aliens? Will they be nice?

Think of the Earth as a spaceship the size of a planet, traveling through the universe at an amazing speed. We are its lucky passengers. We have air to breathe, water to drink, and food to eat, and they all come from the Earth, just like we do. In the past few centuries we have also invented amazing machines, new medicines, and even new ways of thinking. Can we use our inventions for good? Will machines ever truly think? If they can, where will this leave us? How can we take care of the planet, and what will become of it if we ever leave?

These are questions grown-ups ask just as much as children do. Just as we also sit and wonder what the future will be like. Will it be a good one to live in? We would like it to be!

The truth is that it takes each of us and all of us, working together, to figure out what our shared futures will look like. In this book, we have tried to imagine some wonderful worlds, the way the future could look if we try our very hardest. The rest is up to you!

See you in the future.

—Lavie and Richard

Part 1:
EARTH

Earth has been home to humans for hundreds of thousands of years (and animals for millions). Our beautiful blue and green planet is all that we know, but life on Earth is constantly evolving. From intelligent robots, to miracle cures for the sick, and cities that can think for themselves, what's next for the place we call home?

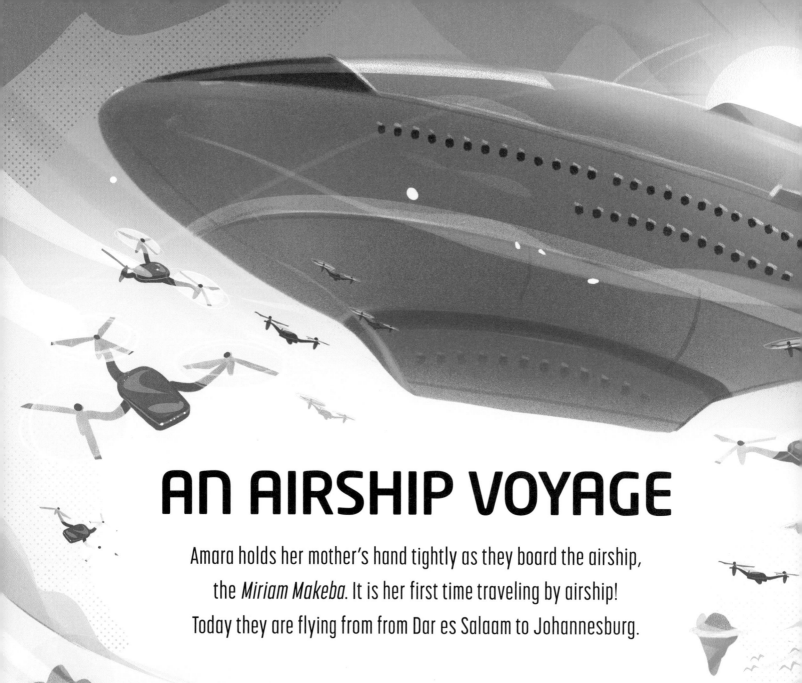

AN AIRSHIP VOYAGE

Amara holds her mother's hand tightly as they board the airship,
the *Miriam Makeba*. It is her first time traveling by airship!
Today they are flying from from Dar es Salaam to Johannesburg.

The giant vessel lifts into the sky.
Amara sees the ocean below,
and the floating islands off the
coast of her homeland, Tanzania.

Soon, the airship settles into its
high altitude. The world below is vast,
but everything seems tiny. Beneath her,
Amara can see a tangle of train tracks
that look like writing. She spots other
airships traveling through the sky and
waves at them, but she doesn't know
if the passengers can see her.

A flock of wild drones joins the
airship. They fly alongside it, before
swooping low on their way to the sea.

Amara says, "Mommy, look!"

But Amara's mother is busy
talking to a work colleague
on the moon, and so Amara
goes to explore the
ship on her own.

A snaillike robot crawls slowly along the floor, leaving a clean path in its trail. A cat slinks past and Amara strokes its head happily. The cat purrs.

"His name is Mkango," a girl says.

Amara knows that means 'lion' in Chichewa.

The girl smiles at Amara. "He's the ship's cat," she explains. She tells Amara that her name is Grace.

"One day I'll be an airship captain too," Grace says, "just like my mom. Come on!"

DID YOU KNOW?

Miriam Makeba was a famous South African singer, also known as Mama Africa.

We are here!

Biomimicry

Robots that imitate animals and insects are already common. Slither bots, for example, are used to crawl through and examine pipes. Copying design ideas found in nature is called biomimicry.

Space rockets

It might be hard to believe, but modern space rockets are the descendants of ideas originated by the ancient Greeks.

The first true rocket was probably a gunpowder-filled firework invented in China around 1232 CE. These 'arrows of flying fire' were originally launched with bows, but people soon found they would fly by themselves when lit.

We are here!

Grace shows Amara around the ship. There is so much to see. In the engine room, engineers feed helium gas into the envelope—a giant balloon overhead that lifts the airship. The engineers control the propellers and the solar-powered engines.

Then Grace takes Amara to the captain's cabin. The view is amazing. The sky is filled with airships, gliders, and balloons. In the distance, Amara can see a space rocket heading up into orbit. Grace's mom even lets Amara pilot the airship herself! If only for a moment.

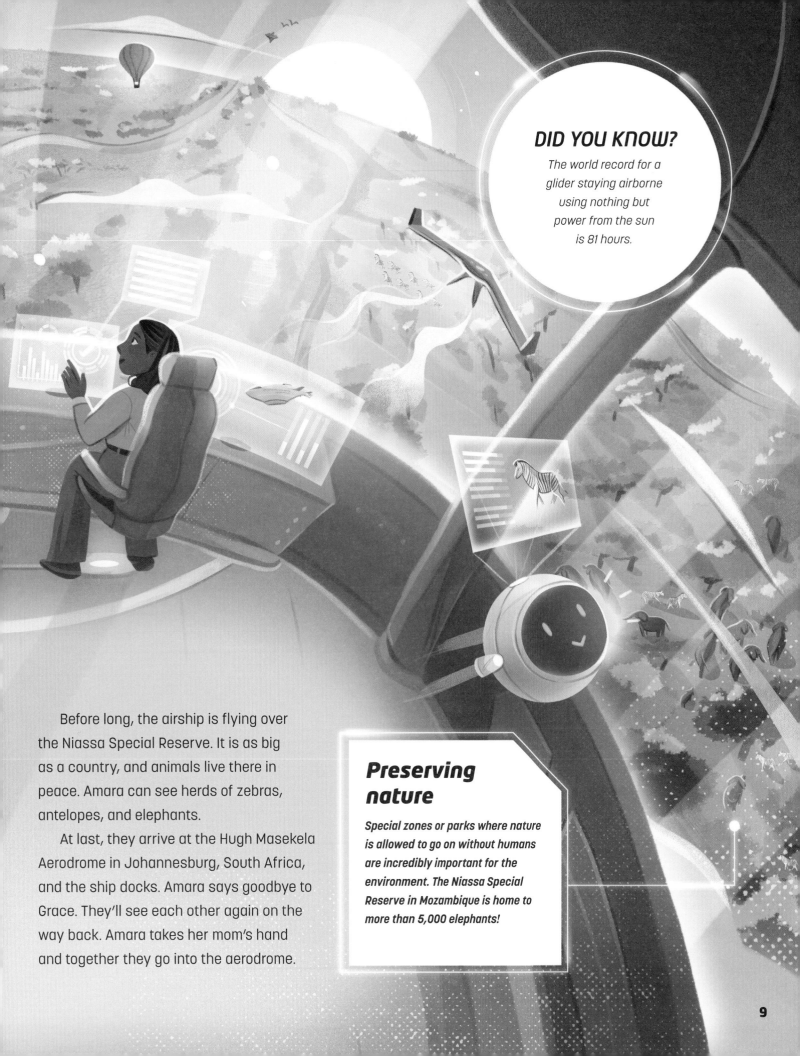

Before long, the airship is flying over the Niassa Special Reserve. It is as big as a country, and animals live there in peace. Amara can see herds of zebras, antelopes, and elephants.

At last, they arrive at the Hugh Masekela Aerodrome in Johannesburg, South Africa, and the ship docks. Amara says goodbye to Grace. They'll see each other again on the way back. Amara takes her mom's hand and together they go into the aerodrome.

Preserving nature

Special zones or parks where nature is allowed to go on without humans are incredibly important for the environment. The Niassa Special Reserve in Mozambique is home to more than 5,000 elephants!

The science of airships

An airship is a motorized aircraft that's lighter than air and able to steer itself. It carries passengers or other loads, and is essentially a giant balloon!

Zeppelins

The most famous airships were called Zeppelins. They were named after the German inventor, Count Ferdinand von Zeppelin.

Making a comeback

Airships became hugely popular in the 1930s. However, the hydrogen gas used to lift them proved highly explosive. After a series of disasters, airships disappeared from the skies, but they are now making a comeback. The helium gas used today is much safer, and airships are far more eco-friendly than passenger planes. Airships the size of 12-story buildings are being built in China and the US, with the expectation that there will be at least 150 of them floating around in 10 years' time.

Rising and falling

This airship is made from a large helium balloon. It has two smaller balloons, called ballonets, that release air to rise, and take in air to descend back to Earth.

Forward ballonet

War and peace

Airships were not always used for peaceful means. During WWI, high-flying airships dropped thousands of bombs over London, causing terrible devastation.

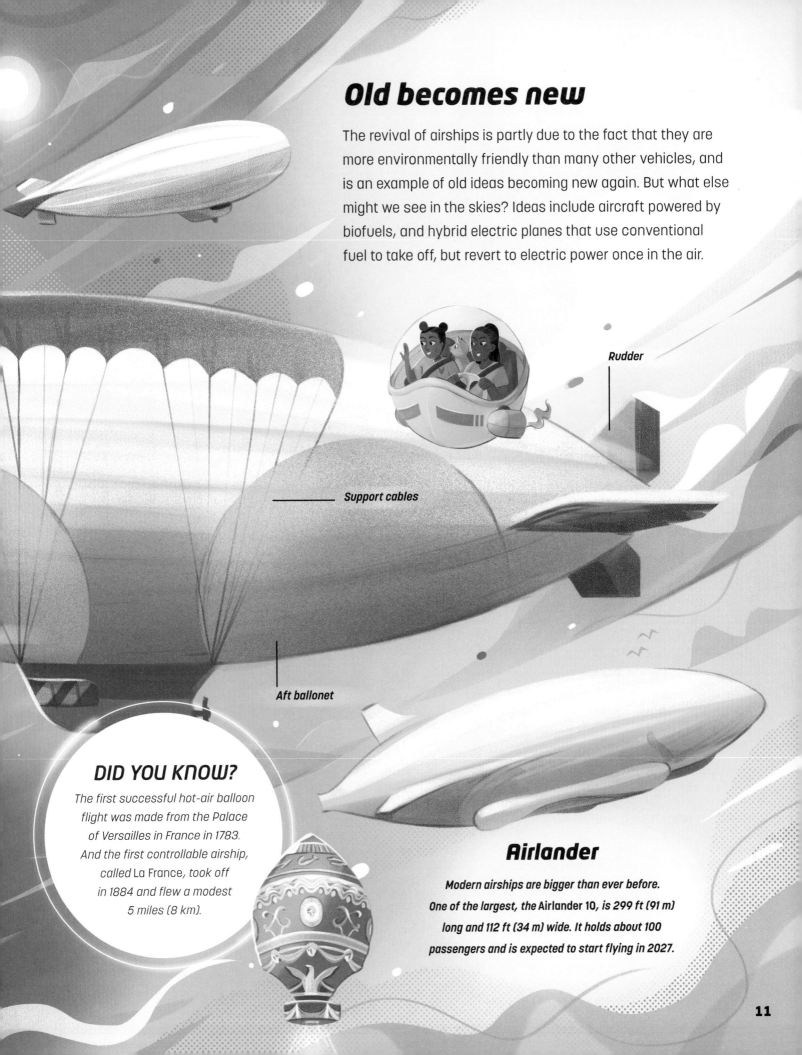

Old becomes new

The revival of airships is partly due to the fact that they are more environmentally friendly than many other vehicles, and is an example of old ideas becoming new again. But what else might we see in the skies? Ideas include aircraft powered by biofuels, and hybrid electric planes that use conventional fuel to take off, but revert to electric power once in the air.

Rudder

Support cables

Aft ballonet

DID YOU KNOW?

The first successful hot-air balloon flight was made from the Palace of Versailles in France in 1783. And the first controllable airship, called La France, took off in 1884 and flew a modest 5 miles (8 km).

Airlander

Modern airships are bigger than ever before. One of the largest, the Airlander 10, is 299 ft (91 m) long and 112 ft (34 m) wide. It holds about 100 passengers and is expected to start flying in 2027.

A DAY IN THE CITY

The sky over Hua Lamphong station is filled with delivery drones and hot-air balloons. Dara and Lek stare in fascination through the window. They'd traveled to Thailand's capital, Bangkok, overnight, on the sleeper train from Nong Khai.

"Look!" Dara points. "A messenger bird!"

Lek stares at the huge creature that swoops through the air with a package in its claws. It is part eagle and part machine, hatched and coded in the Kunming labs in China. Lek watches as the bird neatly avoids collision with a floating restaurant. The diners, who sit in a gondola under a huge hot-air balloon, toss the bird a treat. It snaps it up and vanishes, lost between the green skyscrapers of Old Bangkok. Vertical gardens grow on the sides of the walls, and solar panels catch sunlight and convert it into clean power for the city.

"Come on!" Mom hurries them out of the train. She makes fish robots in Nong Khai that swim in the Mekong River and clean it by eating pollution. "We've lots to do!"

Lek's stomach rumbles as they pass a row of vending machines printing out instant noodles. Outside, the sun shines, and Lek can smell flowering frangipani and jasmine. The street is filled with the shadows of flyers overhead. Solar-powered tuk-tuks glide along the wide avenues outside the station.

Printing food

Scientists are experimenting with growing meat in labs, so it doesn't have to come from animals. Food scientists are also using combinations of soy, chickpeas, and coconut fat to make plant-based, meat-like food! In the future, vending machines printing out quick food on demand could be a common sight in cities.

PLANT-BASED FOOD

It is very hot, but cool air blows from vents in the ground. Monks in saffron robes walk past, laughing. Lek can see delicious food everywhere. Mom buys moo ping meat skewers from a stall and gives them to Lek and Dara. They board a balloon taxi to Ploenchit, where Mom is having a meeting.

Lek looks down on the city. Tall buildings bloom with vibrant greens, while calm blue canals snake between them, and houseboats travel through the water. He can see lots of people, robots, solar panels, drones, and khom loi—buildings floating in the sky like lanterns. Lek loves coming to the big city. There is so much to see and do!

A dandelion flower falls down gently from the sky and Lek catches it. He blows on it and the seeds scatter, all over Bangkok.

UPGRADED AUNT

Juan stops outside the big white building. All around him, ambulances come and go by road and by air, and visitors meet friends and relatives in the large outdoor gardens.

It's paint, but not as we know it

Keeping hospitals sparkling clean and germ-free is really important. One way to do this is to regularly clean surfaces with disinfectant. Another way is to use antibacterial paint. This is a type of paint that kills 99.9 percent of nasty germs!

"I don't want to go in!" Juan says.

"Don't be scared!" Lucia says, laughing. "Aunt Maria is waiting for us."

But Juan is scared of hospitals. It takes his sister a lot of effort to finally drag him in.

Inside, it doesn't smell as bad as Juan feared. In fact, it smells nice and clean! The walls are white and everyone's uniforms are immaculate. They all look very efficient. A robot goes past, wheeling a patient who has his arm in a metal device. The man looks at them and smiles. "They're growing me a new arm," he says.

"See?" Lucia says. "Isn't this fun!"

Juan doesn't think this is fun. Lucia wants to be a doctor when she grows up. Juan wants to design spaceships. But Lucia always tells him that even in space people will need doctors.

Lucia is never wrong. She's just super annoying. Big sisters always are!

Aunt Maria is waiting for them in a hospital room. She smiles happily when she sees them.

"Juan! Lucia! Come give your aunt a kiss."

Juan stares suspiciously at his aunt. She is covered in devices—and she has a new eye!

"Do you like it?" Aunt Maria asks. "I can see in infrared now."

"What are they doing to you?" Juan asks.

"They're just upgrading me, silly!" Aunt Maria says. "I'm getting some of my bones replaced with titanium, and they're injecting me with lots of nanobots to make my immune system stronger."

"I need all of this to go to space, Juan. I'm going to be one of the first people on Mars, helping build a city there. Isn't that cool?"

Juan has to admit it is. Now he's jealous—and sad he won't see Aunt Maria once she goes.

"I'll come back to visit, silly!" she says.

She holds him tight. Juan worries she will crush him with her new strength, but Aunt Maria's hug feels just right.

"See?" Lucia says. "Hospitals aren't all bad!"

"I guess," Juan says. Then he smiles. Next time he gets sick, he won't feel so scared!

Future cities

Just two centuries ago, only a small number of people lived in cities—but that soon changed. Big cities are crowded and noisy, but people love living together. Cities are exciting!

Sizable cities

Today, the majority of people live in large cities. The world's largest city is Tokyo in Japan, where 37 million people live! But soon there will be more than 500 'megacities'—that's a lot of water, food, housing, and transportation! So how can megacities support this? One idea is to make things more local, such as turning skyscrapers into vertical farms to grow crops.

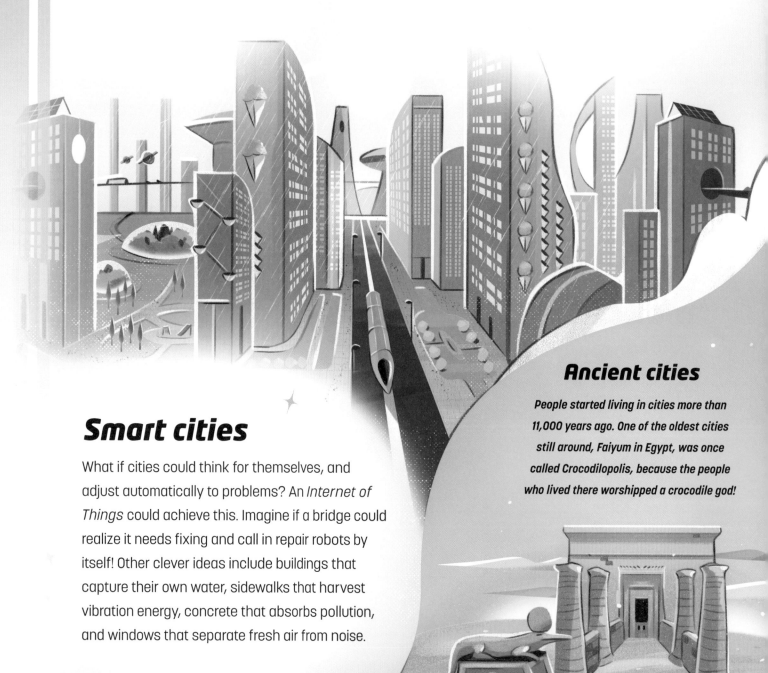

Smart cities

What if cities could think for themselves, and adjust automatically to problems? An *Internet of Things* could achieve this. Imagine if a bridge could realize it needs fixing and call in repair robots by itself! Other clever ideas include buildings that capture their own water, sidewalks that harvest vibration energy, concrete that absorbs pollution, and windows that separate fresh air from noise.

Ancient cities

People started living in cities more than 11,000 years ago. One of the oldest cities still around, Faiyum in Egypt, was once called Crocodilopolis, because the people who lived there worshipped a crocodile god!

Quick haircut or life-saving surgery?

In the olden days, if you needed surgery you had to go to the barber! Barber-surgeons cut hair—and chopped off limbs for a price. This is why barbers, to this day, are known for the red-and-white poles outside their shops. The red is for blood! Try not to think about that the next time you go for a haircut!

Future you

The ideas in *Upgraded Aunt* might sound like sci-fi, and once they were! But these days people have artificial limbs, and bionic eyes and ears. Soon there may be 3D printed bones, spare body parts grown in labs, and contact lenses that connect to the internet!

Cutting-edge cures

In the future, many of today's diseases will disappear, and a visit to the doctor could become very different! For example, your doctor might be an Artificial Intelligence system. Or surgery might be conducted by a robot. Maybe disease will vanish altogether, and microscopic robots called nanobots will be injected into your bloodstream to repair damage.

Hospitals of tomorrow

The history of hospitals goes back a long time. Ancient Greeks were among the first to design public buildings for healing the sick. But in the future, medicine is likely to be transformed by tech. AI systems will suggest treatments, or people might 'wear' doctors on their wrists 24/7. Best of all, tech can be used to stop people becoming sick in the first place!

THE SALVAGERS

The huge Ferris Wheel spins against the darkening skies. It is made of salvaged materials and powered by an old biofuel generator fed with potato peels. The lights come alive all over the fairground. Yves and Benoit are busy helping the grown-ups set everything up.

The carnival travels all across the continent. There is so much stuff left over from the olden days—and so much of it can be reused and repurposed! Their trucks are made out of refashioned refrigerators, ovens, and even toasters. The wheels are recycled rubber and the engines are powered by sunlight, collected every day using foldable sheets that the fairground folks spread out on the ground. Nothing is wasted when you're a salvager!

As Yves' dad always says, "This life is not for everyone, but it is the only life for me!"

Yves couldn't agree more. He loves traveling from place to place and waking up in a new town every day! There is never a boring moment at the carnival. Acrobats juggle ancient phones and gadgets, and the crowds gasp at the high wire above. The strongman smashes everything you give him, reducing plastic to dust so it can be recycled, as no one makes plastic anymore.

The magician takes old stuff and turns it into new things. Yves is an assistant magician.

Minerals in your mobile phone

Did you know that phones contain gold? They also contain other valuable metals including silver, platinum, nickel, and even diamonds. There's also oil, salt, and quartz. Even water is used in the manufacturing process. If you took all the valuable materials from 2,205 lb (1,000 kg) of smartphones, you'd be left with 154 lb (70 kg) of copper, 33 lb (15 kg) of lithium, 2 lb (1 kg) of silver and 0.5 lb (227 g) of gold. That's enough gold to make around 50 gold rings!

"They're almost here!" Benoit says, as he and Yves run to the gates. The crowd is waiting to get in. On the path that leads to the main tent there are lots of stalls, offering food, drinks, and old stuff the salvagers have found. People love old stuff! They also bring their own old things to trade or give away. One tent is reserved for amateur makers, who tinker with junk. Other tents are filled with old books and strange machines.

"Nothing is junk," Yves' dad always says. "Everything has a purpose! And if it doesn't anymore, we give it a new one!"

"Abracadabra!" Yves says. He makes a toy rocket appear. It's a rare toy made on Mars! Somehow it has traveled all the way to Earth.

Yves and Benoit help the grown-ups usher the audience in. Then they go to the glow-in-the-dark cotton candy stand.

Nothing is wasted at the salvagers' fair! Yves and Benoit happily eat their cotton candy until there's nothing left.

DID YOU KNOW?

Around 17% of all food from stores, restaurants, and homes ends up in trash cans. Using vegetable remains for compost is a good way to salvage some of the waste. Or, for those who live in the country, animals such as pigs and chickens are always hungry and happy to help!

Part 2:
LIFE ON LAND AND SEA

Humans have always been fascinated by the unknown, and under the sea is no different. The mystery of what's lurking below the surface has captivated many. But what if we could actually live underwater? Or make new homes for ourselves in floating cities? Could we reside with robots and even talk to plants and animals? Read on to bring these wild and wonderful ideas to life!

THE WILD THAMES

Lucy stands at the front of the boat. The wide Thames opens up before her, its green riverbanks covered in trees that reflect in the water.

Salmon pass below. A heron flies overhead, while another stands still in the shallows, hunting fish. The sun shines and the air is clear. Boats float gently on the water, their solar panels open up to the skies.

Mom is piloting their boat. Dad is fishing off the side. Lucy waits and watches in the early morning light. She can't wait to see Geshem again!

Ahead, a pod of river dolphins play. One of them swims closer. Her dolphin name is too hard for humans to pronounce. Lucy calls her Joy, since she's so joyful!

"Hello, Lucy!" Joy calls, in whistles and clicks.

"Hi, Joy!" Lucy says in English. Joy throws water at her and she jumps, laughing. "Hey! Not fair!"

The boat sails on, with its silent, solar-powered engine.

Aurochs

Aurochs were the last of the megafauna (really big animals). The males were almost 6.5 ft (2 m) high, and they had very long horns! They were huge and cattle-like. They ranged across Asia and Europe from ancient times all the way to the 17th century, when the last one died. Imagine seeing these huge animals wandering around!

DID YOU KNOW?

Dolphins are said to be one of the smartest creatures on the planet, and scientists have been trying to learn their language for a long time.

Forgotten cousins

When our ancient ancestors left Africa, they might have been surprised to discover there were other human species in other places! Among them were the Neanderthals, who lived about 400,000 years ago. We know some of them got along with our ancestors— and many people today still have a little Neanderthal DNA in them! The last Neanderthals went extinct around 40,000 years ago, along with all the other human species, such as the Denisovans, who lived predominantly in Asia.

The trees thin on the Richmond side of the river and Lucy sees a herd of majestic aurochs. Their horns glint in the sunlight, as they wander the grounds of Ham House. The last auroch died in the 17th century, but aurochs were brought back to life by geneticists in this new, gentler England.

Soon, Lucy can see Eel Pie Island rise in the middle of the river. It is covered in ancient woodland: pine, ash, beech, and oak. But dominating them all is the Great Oak, rising from the heart of the small island and towering into the skies. Wood and bamboo houses hang from its branches. The boat arrives at the shore and Lucy hops out. Her friend Geshem is waiting for her. They smile and wave.

Geshem is a neo-Neanderthal. Lucy knows that the Neanderthals were a human species who lived in Europe and Asia long before the arrival of modern humans. But they died out many thousands of years ago. Then scientists brought them back to life from ancient DNA.

"Let's climb!" Geshem says.

They run to the Great Oak and climb up it until they reach one of the wide branches at the top. From up here, they can see so much! The sun catches the water and an eagle soars overhead. *All the things that were once extinct are alive again*, Lucy thinks happily. She holds Geshem's hand and, laughing, they ride a slide that transports them back down to the river!

THE WORLDWIDE WOOD

"Hello, Kwame," the Wood whispers.
"Hello... hello... hello..."
"Hello, Wood!" Kwame says.

Kwame looks to his father for confirmation. "Do I call it Wood?"

"You're looking in the wrong place," his father says. "Look down."

Kwame looks at the deep rich earth, covered in leaves. "What's under there?"

The Wood laughs. Its laughter is the sound of rain falling, roots growing, insects buzzing, and birds singing. It is very beautiful.

Mindful mushrooms

Scientists once thought that only animals with big brains could feel things, or think for themselves. We now know that lots of species, from tiny trees to giant whales, are aware of their surroundings and can communicate with each other, often sharing resources. Some animal species—notably apes, dolphins, whales, and octopuses—are sentient, meaning they are aware and able to experience feelings.

They are deep inside the wood, where Kwame's father studies mushrooms.

"I'm here," the Wood says. "I'm underneath!"

Kwame looks. Not with his eyes, but with his mind, which is connected to the Gaia—the Internet of Everything.

Below him the wood is a tangled, complex mass resembling a human brain. Amongst its roots, thin threads extend for miles, connected to everything.

"That's the mycelium," Kwame's father tells him. "Mycelium are fungus threads."

The Wood whispers in contentment. Kwame reaches deeper with his mind and feels a shock of recognition. There is a consciousness down there!

It isn't like a human mind, but it feels warm and welcoming. The Wood shows Kwame the deep dreams of roots and fungi. There are machines too, now, connected to the Worldwide Wood, helping translate its thoughts into human thoughts.

A living world?

Evolutionary biologist Lynn Margulis and futurist James Lovelock wrote about their belief that the entire planet works as a single, self-regulating system. Some people even propose that the Earth itself is conscious, and we are all just a small part of this planetary mind!

"I am old, Kwame," the Wood says. "Here, trees and fungi have always been present. We talk to each other. In the old days all we talked about was survival. But now we talk to people. Isn't that wonderful? Now we get to dream."

"What do you dream about?" Kwame asks.

"I dream about growing on the Moon. And on Mars. I dream of growing everywhere people go."

"I don't want to go to Mars," Kwame says. "I like it here just fine!"

"Me too," the Wood says. It laughs happily.

Kwame and his father walk hand in hand through the radiant forest.

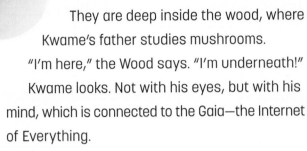

DID YOU KNOW?

The term 'Worldwide Wood' (or wood wide web) was coined by scientist, Dr Suzanne Simard. She discovered that trees talk to each other, and even work together, using an underground network of fungi. How cool is that!

Life on Earth

We assume as humans that we are at the top of the evolutionary tree, and have reached some kind of peak. This is not necessarily true. If by misfortune, accident, or stupidity, humans cease to exist, chances are life on Earth will go on and continue to evolve!

Back to the wild

The idea of a natural landscape seems simple—trees, grass, and animals. But in reality, humans have been changing land for a long time! A hillside may seem untouched, but could have been an ancient forest before it was cleared for agriculture. Equally, many plants and animals we think are natural have been selectively bred for years.

What could be next?

Will the future be the age of the ants, apes, or trees? Or will humans remain Earth's dominant species? Maybe we'll merge with machines and replace our bodies with yet to be invented technology! Or could we embrace a simpler life? The most likely scenario could be a mix of the two. In the face of AI, we might focus on what's human, and value craft and tradition, and also seek solace in the natural world—sometimes using technology to achieve it!

Rewilding and conserving

The idea of returning landscapes to a more wild state has already captured people's imaginations. Rewilding includes conserving wilderness areas and restoring biodiversity by replanting trees and plants, and reintroducing previously common animals.

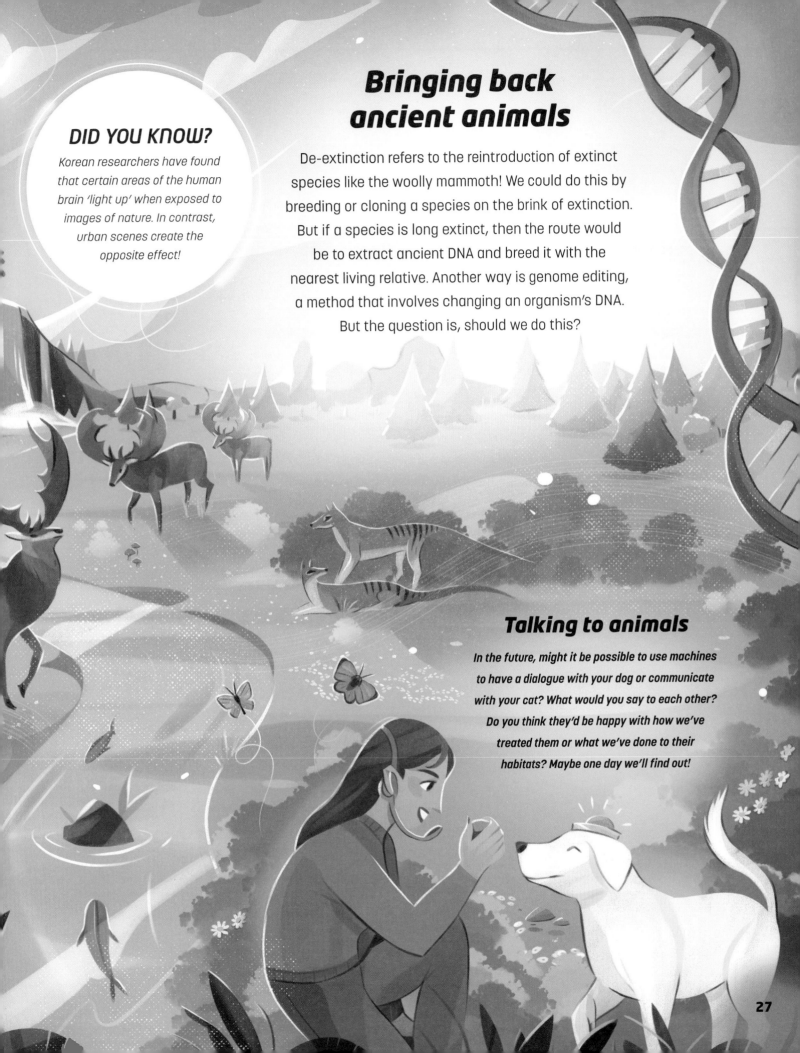

Bringing back ancient animals

De-extinction refers to the reintroduction of extinct species like the woolly mammoth! We could do this by breeding or cloning a species on the brink of extinction. But if a species is long extinct, then the route would be to extract ancient DNA and breed it with the nearest living relative. Another way is genome editing, a method that involves changing an organism's DNA. But the question is, should we do this?

DID YOU KNOW?

Korean researchers have found that certain areas of the human brain 'light up' when exposed to images of nature. In contrast, urban scenes create the opposite effect!

Talking to animals

In the future, might it be possible to use machines to have a dialogue with your dog or communicate with your cat? What would you say to each other? Do you think they'd be happy with how we've treated them or what we've done to their habitats? Maybe one day we'll find out!

OUR NEW NONHUMAN FRIENDS

"Can you help me?" Saad says. "I think I'm lost."

"Oh, no!" the robot says. He's a very curious robot. He looks like a giant grasshopper. Saad can't see any other humans. But there are a lot of robots!

Some of them look like cars, others like birds, and one slithers along the road, humming to itself. Some of the robots look like people. But Saad can't see his parents, or anyone that isn't a robot.

"I will help you," the curious robot says. "My name is Artemis. I've never met a human before!"

The robot takes Saad's hand with its front leg. It feels warm and metallic.

"Let's find your parents!" Artemis says.

They walk through town. It is a robot town, situated in an area where a large robot population resides. It's on the Kamchatka Peninsula, near the Bering Sea. It gets very cold in the winter, but the robots are equipped to deal with the weather!

Soon they come to a large intersection where robots on wheels and tracks go whooshing past. Artemis takes Saad to a huge robot that looks like a vending machine.

"This is M.I.N.E.R.V.A," Artemis says. "She is a very old AI. She was here even before they built Lunar Port on the moon!"

"Hello, Minerva," Saad says shyly.

"Hello, Saad!" Minerva booms. "Your parents are worried about you!" She laughs kindly. "They are waiting for you at the Old Robots Home. Artemis will take you. Is that all right?"

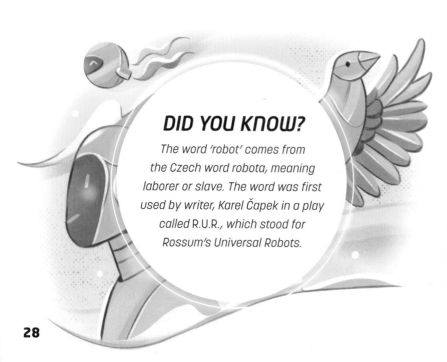

DID YOU KNOW?

The word 'robot' comes from the Czech word robota, meaning laborer or slave. The word was first used by writer, Karel Čapek in a play called R.U.R., which stood for Rossum's Universal Robots.

"Thank you, Minerva!" Saad says. He follows Artemis through a bewildering array of smart buildings.

Between them, crawling, hopping, and running robots of all shapes and sizes play a game of soccer. They stop and stare when they see the human boy.

"Come play! Join us!" they cry.

"Later, later," Artemis says importantly.

Before long, they arrive at beautiful gardens, with manicured lawns and flowers. Sitting on the grass are the oldest robots Saad has ever seen. They are taken care of by people.

Saad sees his mom and dad. He runs to them and they hug him, happy and relieved.

"Saad, this is Daisy, who took care of me when I was young." She gestures to a small humanoid robot.

"Hello, Saad," Daisy says softly. She is old and covered in rust spots. "It's lovely to meet you at last."

Saad says hello, and then asks if he can go and play soccer with the other robots.

Everyone laughs because it sounds like Saad thinks he is *also* a robot now.

Mom tells him that of course he can. "Just don't forget to come back for dinner!"

Saad runs away happily, with Artemis hopping beside him. They're just in time to join the soccer game!

Robot soccer

Can robots play soccer? Yes, they can! Players aren't quite as good as Cristiano Ronaldo or Lionel Messi yet, but robot soccer is an official sport, which began in South Korea in 1995. The Robot Football World Cup, or RoboCup, features different leagues, and the aim is to design robots that can win matches against humans by 2050.

Da Vinci

The famous artist, engineer, and scientist, Leonardo da Vinci, designed mechanical robots in the forms of a lion and a knight. Although as far as we know, neither were ever actually built.

Elektro (and Sparko)

In 1939, a robot named Elektro was exhibited at the New York World's Fair. Many other robots followed, most of which were bipedal—they had two legs and usually two arms too. They all looked a little bit like us!

Tesla

Inventor, Nikola Tesla, built a remote control boat in 1898, which some say was the world's first drone. It was also the first known use of wireless remote control technology.

Sparko

Robots

Robots have their origins in mechanical toys called 'automata'. The ancient Greeks, Persians, Mesopotamians, Indians, and Chinese all designed mechanical devices.

Pros and cons

The things humans find easy tend to be the stuff that robots find hard to do. This is still true for most robots. They are often designed to do just one thing, such as carry bags, climb stairs, or cut grass. But things are changing...

Robot lawn mower

Wabot-1

In the 1960s, the first industrial robots appeared in factories. Then in 1972, a professor named Ichiro Kato designed the world's first full-scale android (robot with human appearance). WABOT-1 was able to walk, grip items, and 'see' using two cameras.

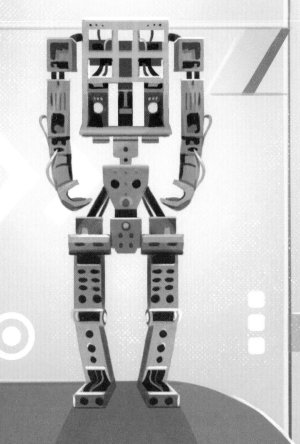

Rise of the robots

In the future, it's likely that robots will far outnumber people. They will be commonplace too, not hidden in factories or water pipes. You will see robots delivering pizza, carrying groceries, flying helicopters, caring for sick people, or just hanging around with their owners. As to whether robots will ever be able to truly have a conversation with people, that's hard to say. They will probably do a pretty good job though! The question won't really be what can a robot do, but rather, what can't they do? Perhaps the bigger question is, what shouldn't robots be allowed to do?

All kinds of robots

When people think about robots they often imagine humanoid machines that are up to no good. But there are many types of helpful robots, including PARO the seal, that helps to care for elderly people, and PaPeRo (stands for Partner-type-Personal-Robot), a childcare robot. Most robots today are not humanoid at all. For example, car factories use robotic machines to build vehicles.

PaPeRo

PARO the seal

AFLOAT AT SEA

The hot wind carries the tang of salt and tar. Mei stands on the shore and watches Oceanus City float in the warm waters of the bay. It bobs in the sea. A city of low-lying buildings, wide avenues, and palm trees.

City workers lay down gently swaying gangways which lead from the city to the shore. As soon as they anchor, Mei sees her friend Silvia running toward her, waving and shouting, "Mei! Mei!"

"Silvia!" Mei says as they hug. It's so good to see each other! Mei follows Silvia along a gangway into the city. There are beautiful parks and open-air swimming pools that are simply the sea! They go swimming and have ice cream, and eat fresh fish on the grill for dinner.

They wake up early the next morning to see the city go out to sea. The crew pull up the heavy anchor and roll back the gangways—and they're off! The city moves slowly away from the land.

Testing the waters

There is a glimpse of a possible future in Amsterdam, the capital of the Netherlands. Around 100 homes float on the water there in a part of the city called IJburg. The Netherlands has a long experience of building sea walls and dykes to stop the low-lying lands reclaimed from the sea from flooding. Lots of Dutch people also live on houseboats on the many canals.

Everyone goes to the promenade to throw lines into the sea. Mei can't believe how many fish there are!

The city floats until the shore is far behind them. The next day they see another city in the distance. It's the city of Oshun. It has sails and tall towers that capture rainwater, and solar panels that gleam in the hot sun. Everyone waves—from a distance!

"Look!" Mei says. "Whales!" She has never seen them before. Silvia laughs at her surprise. The whales rise, as enormous as mountains. They blow water into the air in greeting!

There is so much life out at sea. They see other towns floating, and huge seaweed farms.

They often see people traveling by boat. In the early mornings people go out with sky gliders to catch the wind, and travel above them like birds!

"I never want to go back," Mei says. "Living on the sea is the best!"

"Well, I like it," Silvia says, and they laugh.

Mei is so glad she got to visit her friend. They both cannot wait for their next adventure together!

DID YOU KNOW?

Bangladesh is home to a series of floating gardens that move up and down with the waters. It is also home to several solar-powered, 'boat schools' that float!

JOURNEY TO THE BOTTOM OF THE SEA

One day, Mei sees a huge structure rise out of the sea far in the distance. It is like a beautiful glass and metal dome, and when the sunlight catches it, it breaks into rainbows!

"What's that?" Mei asks.

"That's the Spiral," Silvia says. "It's an underwater city—one of the oldest!"

"Can we visit it?" Mei asks excitedly.

"Of course! My friend Jabulani lives there."

Oceanus City anchors away from the Spiral. By now, Mei is used to the way the city operates. Silvia's dad takes them to the passenger boat, and they board with all the other visitors to the Spiral. As they approach, Mei can see all the way down through the clean water! The Spiral starts off as a huge sphere, like a ball submerged under the surface. But below it, the city continues in a long corkscrew shape, all the way to the bottom of the sea! When they dock, they go inside the sphere, and then down. Mei looks through the walls to the outside. She can see fish, divers, and submarines traveling up and down. Inside it is warm. The air is clear and there are lots of trees and plants.

"Hi, Silvia and Mei!" a boy says. It's Jabulani!

"Can I show you my favorite place on the Spiral?"

A fuel (and food) of the future?

Seaweed is extraordinary! It uses energy from sunlight (even when deep underwater) to take nutrients and carbon dioxide from sea water. It can be eaten, used to make biofuel, fertilizer, sustainable plastic; is found in pet food, toothpaste, medicines, makeup; and can even fight climate change! Wow! Scientists are now trying to grow seaweed in tanks on land.

Mei agrees eagerly. There is so much to see! There are fish and seaweed farms, and all kinds of fun excursions to go diving and sailing and swimming. But Jabulani takes them down in an elevator to the lower levels. It's different here, where the sunlight can barely reach. Mei can see a pod of whales in the inky dark.

"They sing to each other," Jabulani says. "Whale song can travel for miles and miles under the sea!"

They stop and listen. It is both eerie and beautiful.

"This isn't what I want to show you, though," Jabulani says. He takes them even deeper, where they can't see the sea anymore. The pressure is enormous outside, and it's a bit like being inside a spaceship.

"There!" he says, pointing to a doorway that leads to a viewing platform with screens. It shows them a sphere, floating like an egg in the deep, dark sea.

"What is it?" Mei asks in awe.

"It's where the Deep Ones live," Jabulani says. "They're very old AI. The cold of the sea makes them run fast, and it's safe and comfortable for them here. They think deep thoughts—get it?" They all laugh.

"But what do they think about?" Mei asks.

The answer comes faintly, from the walls, like an echo. *We think about you... you... you...*

Mei can feel the Deep Ones' love and happiness.

And we like to listen to the whale song... song... song... the Deep Ones continue.

"So cool!" Mei says. "Can we get ice cream now?"

Jabulani laughs. "Yes, I'd love an ice cream too!"

*Ice cream...*the Deep Ones say happily.

Mei laughs. The three of them go back in the elevator, to the sunlight of the upper layers. They have delicious durian ice cream—but Mei thinks about the Deep Ones, and she will do for a long time to come. She thinks, maybe one day she could visit them again, and they could listen to the music of the sea together!

DID YOU KNOW?

Whales communicate by sound just like we do—but their voices carry out for thousands of miles under the sea! It's a very eerie sound—at least to human ears!

Underwater machines

Deep-sea server farms already exist. They use eco-friendly power sources and are filled with dry nitrogen in sealed containers, meaning humans can't go in. The coldness underwater helps the computers work. The farms are also close to shore so they can be used quickly and reliably.

Water worlds

The idea of underwater living became popular in 1870, due to the book *Twenty Thousand Leagues Under the Sea* by Jules Verne. It took almost a century to carry out the first real-world experiments, but now they are happening more!

The Spiral

The idea of the Spiral isn't new. Ocean Spiral is a Japanese concept, where up to 5,000 people could live underwater by 2030. But how might this work in terms of providing the necessary energy, water, food, and essential services?

A city with a twist

One of the earliest underwater habitats was *Conshelf II,* a starfish-shaped village 33 ft (10 m) deep in the Red Sea, built by famous oceanographer Jacques Cousteau in 1963. It housed 'oceanauts' who lived completely underwater for up to a month at a time!

Spiral-shaped wind turbines

Base station tethered to the seabed

Living on the water

As well as living underwater, living *on* the water is another popular idea. The Ma'dan are inhabitants of the Mesopotamian marshlands in modern day Iraq and Iran. Most of them used to live in houses made from reeds located on riverbanks, or on artificial islands also made of reeds. Lake Titicaca, on the border of Peru and Bolivia, is similarly home to a series of floating reed islands.

DID YOU KNOW?

Some people get married underwater! And NASA even uses underwater environments to simulate the effects of space—especially zero gravity.

Why aren't there more floating cities?

Two reasons for this are practicality and security. It's often easier to make an artificial island than a floating one. Anything that floats is more at risk of sinking or damage from extreme weather. There are advantages to building on water though—water generally remains cooler than land in summer and warmer than land in winter.

A letter from the sea

The world's only underwater post office lies off the shore of Port Vila in Vanuatu. You can buy a special waterproof postcard, fill it out, and just dive straight down to mail it!

Part 3:

WELCOME TO THE SOLAR SYSTEM

What does the future hold for life in our solar system? Will we build a home for ourselves on the moon, or visit Venus and create cities up in its clouds? Perhaps we'll make it to Mars and move in, or travel through the asteroid belt on a never-ending journey? The possibilities are endless, but one question remains the same: what will we find when we get there?

THE JUNK COLLECTOR

The cloud of junk around Earth glitters like diamonds as it catches the sunlight. "But one person's junk is another person's treasure," Amir's mom says. It's what she always says. Amir's mom is a junk collector. It's a very important job!

Amir stares out the shuttle's window at the sky in low Earth orbit. It is filled with satellites, habitats, and space stations. There are hotels and spaceships teeming with life. Shuttles dart like fireflies and vehicles depart to the moon, Mars, and the cloud cities of Venus. Near-Earth space is amazing!

It is also filled with discarded rocket boosters, broken satellites, and all kinds of debris. Everything people have ever put up in space. Some of it crashes back down to Earth. But a lot of it stays in orbit, and it can be very dangerous.

"There!" Amir says, pointing to the old satellite.

His mother adjusts their route. Their shuttle approaches the orbiting device. They move around Earth as they do so, and the continents shift below them.

A graveyard for spaceships

Many space stations, rocket boosters, and satellites are sent back down to Earth at the end of their working life. They end up in a deep part of the South Pacific Ocean, in a place called the Spacecraft Cemetery, or, more officially, the South Pacific Oceanic Uninhabited Area. There are almost 300 space vehicles buried there.

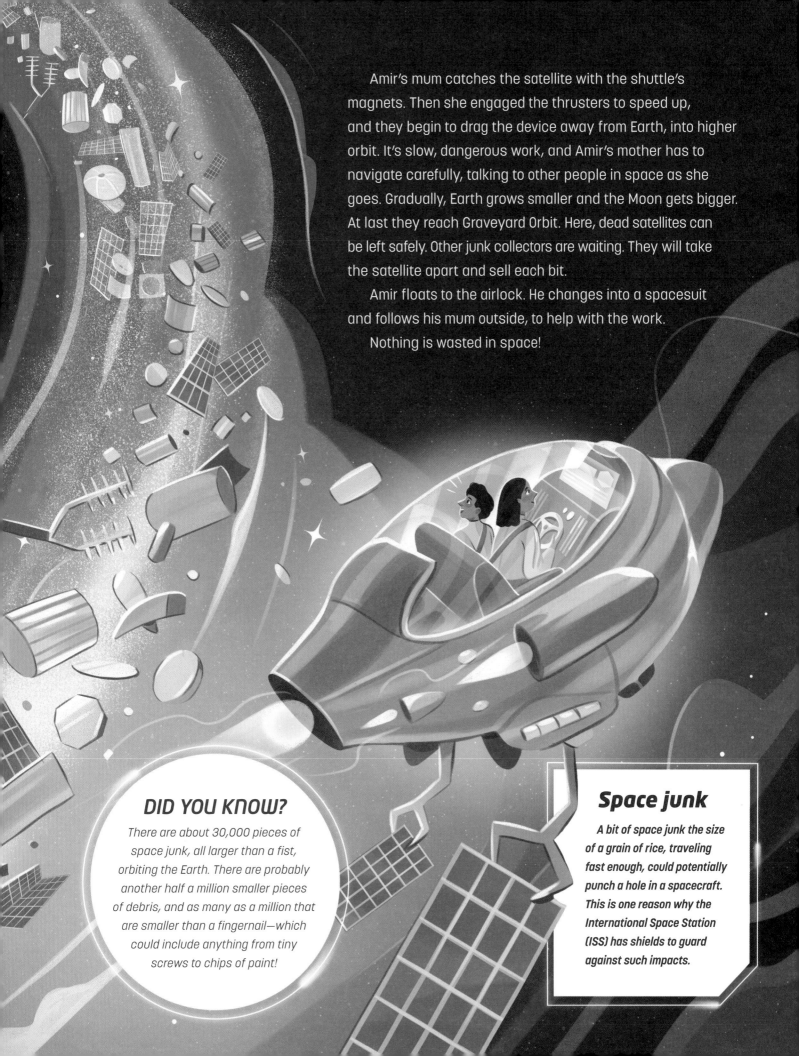

Amir's mum catches the satellite with the shuttle's magnets. Then she engaged the thrusters to speed up, and they begin to drag the device away from Earth, into higher orbit. It's slow, dangerous work, and Amir's mother has to navigate carefully, talking to other people in space as she goes. Gradually, Earth grows smaller and the Moon gets bigger. At last they reach Graveyard Orbit. Here, dead satellites can be left safely. Other junk collectors are waiting. They will take the satellite apart and sell each bit.

Amir floats to the airlock. He changes into a spacesuit and follows his mum outside, to help with the work.

Nothing is wasted in space!

DID YOU KNOW?

There are about 30,000 pieces of space junk, all larger than a fist, orbiting the Earth. There are probably another half a million smaller pieces of debris, and as many as a million that are smaller than a fingernail—which could include anything from tiny screws to chips of paint!

Space junk

A bit of space junk the size of a grain of rice, traveling fast enough, could potentially punch a hole in a spacecraft. This is one reason why the International Space Station (ISS) has shields to guard against such impacts.

Cleaning up

We could clean up the trash we've left in space by using giant nets to catch it like fish! Or we might use giant magnets, or even lasers, to blast the trash out of orbit and back to Earth. Here it could burn up as it enters our atmosphere, or fall into oceans or remote regions where trash robots can pick it up. Trash robots are robots that collect garbage, not robots that aren't very good at their jobs!

Recycle and upcycle

Recycling is good for the environment and cuts carbon dioxide emissions enormously. Recycling reduces the need for raw materials, but it still requires water and energy. That's unless we can locally repurpose materials into new objects—known as upcycling.

Always take your trash home

Humans have been sending things into space for a long time, but we've also been leaving our trash behind, including rockets and dead satellites. This waste can cause problems, so scientists are thinking about ways to clean up this mess.

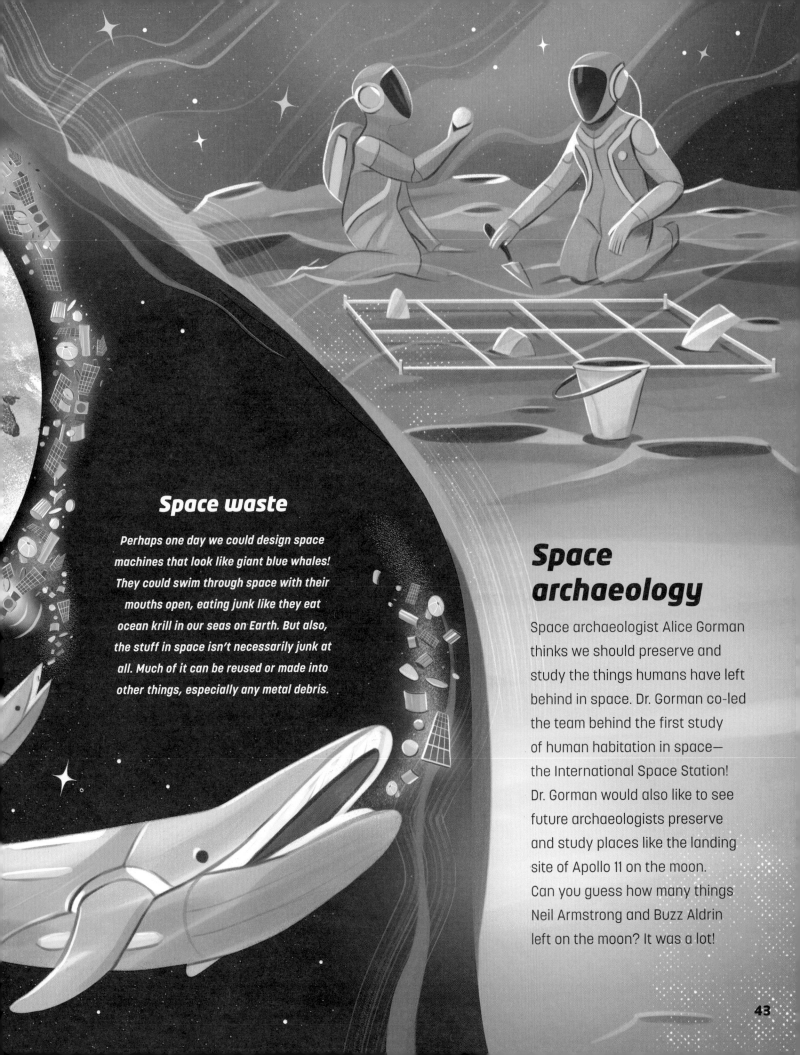

Space waste

Perhaps one day we could design space machines that look like giant blue whales! They could swim through space with their mouths open, eating junk like they eat ocean krill in our seas on Earth. But also, the stuff in space isn't necessarily junk at all. Much of it can be reused or made into other things, especially any metal debris.

Space archaeology

Space archaeologist Alice Gorman thinks we should preserve and study the things humans have left behind in space. Dr. Gorman co-led the team behind the first study of human habitation in space—the International Space Station! Dr. Gorman would also like to see future archaeologists preserve and study places like the landing site of Apollo 11 on the moon. Can you guess how many things Neil Armstrong and Buzz Aldrin left on the moon? It was a lot!

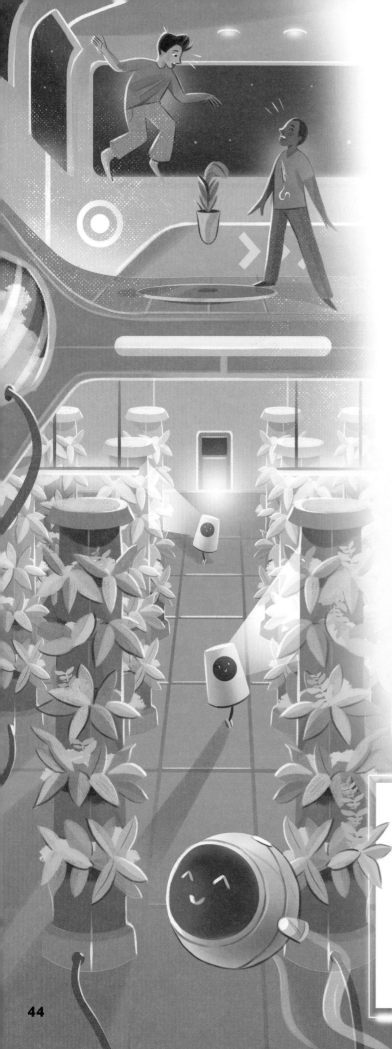

PEAKS OF ETERNAL LIGHT

"Why is everything so weird on the moon?"
Yi-Sheng asks. Yi-Sheng has just arrived from
Earth and he has so many questions!

"Why is the sun always in the sky?" Yi-Sheng asks.
"Why can I jump so high?"

Thabo feels a bit sorry for Yi-Sheng. He doesn't
even know anyone yet! "You will get used to it," Thabo
tells him, laughing despite himself. It's just that Earth kids
are so strange! Everyone knows it's always sunny on the
moon. At least, if you live in the North Pole, on a peak of
eternal light. The peak juts out on the rim of the Peary
Crater, so the sun always shines down on it! The sun
also provides all the energy that Lunar Port needs.
It is the biggest and oldest city on the moon.

"Come on," Thabo says kindly. "I'll show you around!"
Yi-Sheng came on the ship from Earth with his mom
and dad—an engineer and a chef. It's hard cooking on
the moon, but there are lots of fresh vegetables from
the underground hydroponic gardens.

The moon goddess
who sprouted leaves

*The first plant to ever grow on the moon was a tiny seed of cotton.
It was carried on the Chinese spacecraft Chang'e 4, named after the
Chinese moon goddess. The cotton seed sprouted two green leaves.
It was part of an important experiment to see if we could grow plants
on the moon. Perhaps one day flowers will grow there, too!*

Moondust

Lunar dust is a little like powdered glass—and it can be very dangerous! It can erode metal, clog vital air filters, and destroy spacesuits if exposed for too long. And if you breathe it in, like the Apollo astronauts did when they brought some of it back on board on the soles of their feet, it won't be very pleasant either! Future moon missions will need to design special materials to withstand moondust—or we could build moonbases underground, where they won't be exposed to it as much.

DID YOU KNOW?

Under the moon's gray surface layer is the lunar soil. It has a texture a bit like snow—and it smells like gunpowder!

There is so much dust on the moon that most of Lunar Port is built underground. Thabo takes Yi-Sheng to the viewing platform at the very top of the port. The sun feels so nice on their skin! Yi-Sheng watches in awe as the sun lights up the vast crater below. He can see buggies driving around the huge structures of the water mines. He can also see the other peaks around the crater, and the towns built on them, all bathing in eternal light.

Maybe the moon is not so bad, he thinks. He smiles at Thabo, who smiles back. Yi-Sheng is glad to have made a new friend.

BIRTHDAY ON VENUS

Samit wakes up early. He rushes to the window. The roiling red clouds of Venus drift past below. Today is his birthday!

Airships fly by in the distance, ferrying passengers between the cloud cities. But the biggest and best is Tereshkova Port. It is where Samit was born and where he lives. And today he is having a party!

Tereshkova Port is the oldest cloud city. It was built long ago, when people first came to live above Venus. Only machines live on the surface below, where the air is poison and the gravity crushing. But up in the atmosphere, the very air Samit breathes also lifts the city above the clouds. He runs to visit his grandfather in his garden.

"Happy birthday, Samit!" Grandpa Vishal says. He gives Samit a hug. Samit loves visiting his grandfather. Grandpa Vishal's roses are famous throughout the solar system. But his pride and joy is the Black Tereshkova Rose. Samit spends an hour helping in the garden.

Clean air

In 2018, moss-covered benches were installed in cities across Europe, with the ability to absorb as much pollution as a small forest! Perhaps in the future we will see moss-covered buildings, pollution absorbing cement or paint, or even pollution absorbing jeans!

Tereshkova Port is full of beautiful trees and flowers. They help produce the air that the people need. Grandpa Vishal takes Samit for a birthday lunch at the top of the city.

From here, they can see for miles! Samit's mom calls. She is an engineer, and she's been asked to fix one of the water catchers which float above the city. These machines collect precious water from Venus's acid rain.

"I won't be long!" Mom says. Dad joins her in the picture. He is a pilot, and his job is to fly engineers in his blimp. Mom and Dad have fun, but Samit wants to be a gardener when he grows up.

Next, Samit goes to visit his sister, Vandana. She is hooked up to a console and Samit plugs in next to her, to watch. Vandana controls a robot that runs along the surface of Venus. One day, she wants to visit the surface of the planet herself, but it is dangerous for humans!

Everybody comes to Samit's party. Even Aunt Lavanya, who lives in distant Sharma Town, which floats over the North Pole, came especially. Happy birthday, Samit!

Catching rain

The rain on Venus is made of acid! But there is water in the acid, and so scientists propose catching and filtering the Venusian rain to provide water for the cloud cities.

DID YOU KNOW?

Valentina Tereshkova was the first woman in space. She flew on her own and spent 3 days in orbit before landing back on Earth.

Life on the moon

While liquid water can't exist on the surface of the moon due to radiation, water vapor has been detected, as well as signs that water once existed. It's also believed there may be frozen water underground. If found, this would increase the chances of humans living on the moon.

One small step for a mouse

Most people know that astronaut Neil Armstrong was the first human to set foot on the moon, but did you know that in 1972, Apollo 17 carried five mice onboard? Their names were Fe, Fi, Fo, Fum, and Phooey. Though they didn't land, they orbited the moon in the command module for six days before going back to Earth!

Living underground

Have you ever wondered why the moon has so many holes? Most of these craters were made millions of years ago by asteroid strikes! Living on the moon would require protection from cosmic rays and meteoroid impacts. This might mean living in underground cities connected by tunnels that contain vacuum tube trains for high-speed travel.

Resources

Water could come from deep ice mines, and light from nano-solar panels on the moon's surface.

Food on the moon

As for food, it would be relatively easy to grow if you had water and light and used hydroponics. Chances are that moon gardens growing fruit and vegetables would be found in underground caves or covered craters.

Out of this world

The space age started in 1957 with the launch of the Russian satellite *Sputnik 1*. By 1961 the Russians had launched a man into space. In 1969 the Americans landed a man on the moon, and by the 1980s space travel was more common. Fast forward to the 21st century and citizens from 42 countries have been to space!

Getting to Venus

Earth's neighbour Venus is 260 million km (162 million miles) away, which is a very long way. But could trips be made shorter by adding propulsion systems to planets and moving them somewhere more convenient? Impossible? That's what someone once said about heavier-than-air flight!

The future of space travel

How long will it be before the first child is born in space? It will probably happen in your lifetime! Other firsts might include the first person on Mars, the first human to never breathe the Earth's air, and even the first hamburger grown in space!

Finding water

Water is the most precious natural resource on Earth and yet around 2 billion people still don't have access to clean water. In the future, water could be pulled out of thin air using condensation pipes that go underground. Or, if humans live in space where water is scarce, it may be harvested from passing comets or shipped from Earth in vast space tankers.

Living on Venus?

The surface of this planet is extremely hot, so how could humans ever live there? The answer may be to live above it. The atmosphere is quite hospitable if you go 30 miles (48 km) up. Simply attach a giant balloon to a building and it would float in space.

A TRAIN RIDE ON MARS

Adam and Ma'ayan wait at the train station. The dome of the city rises overhead. Tong Yun is the biggest and oldest city on Mars. Most of it is underground.

There are people and robots of all shapes and sizes around. Visiting the train station is always exciting, but especially today, because Adam and Ma'ayan are going to visit their grandmother in the Valles Marineris. It's a long way away!

"Hello, Ma'ayan!" the train says. "Hello, Adam!"

"Hello, train!" Ma'ayan says, smiling brightly. They get on and find their seats. Ma'ayan loves trains. They run all over Mars. Soon, this one is in motion. It's slow at first, as it goes out through the airlock. Then it speeds up into the Martian sands.

Catch that train!

Trains on Mars won't look that different than the ones we're used to, but they would be sealed to hold in fresh air and a human-breathable atmosphere—so don't go opening a window! Iron is plentiful on Mars, and mining for iron could help build railroad lines across the planet, connecting distant points together.

There is plenty to see. Other trains snake out in all directions. The trains have brains of their own. Some people say they all take off once a year and meet somewhere in the desert, to do things only trains do. Ma'ayan wonders if trains dream. What do they dream about? She sees a robot outside the window, metal-detecting for old relics. Mars is littered with the remnants of cheap spaceships and satellites, which crashed here in the early days. She sees a mining rig, its enormous shafts dug down into the ground to extract the precious Martian ice that makes water and air.

"I'm hungry!" Adam says. A flock of drones pass overhead as Adam and Ma'ayan dig into a lunch of rice, fish, and kimchi. The fish are raised in giant vats underground, as large as oceans. The rice and cabbage grow in the Valles Marineris, where Grandma lives. Everyone knows Martian cabbage is the *best* cabbage!

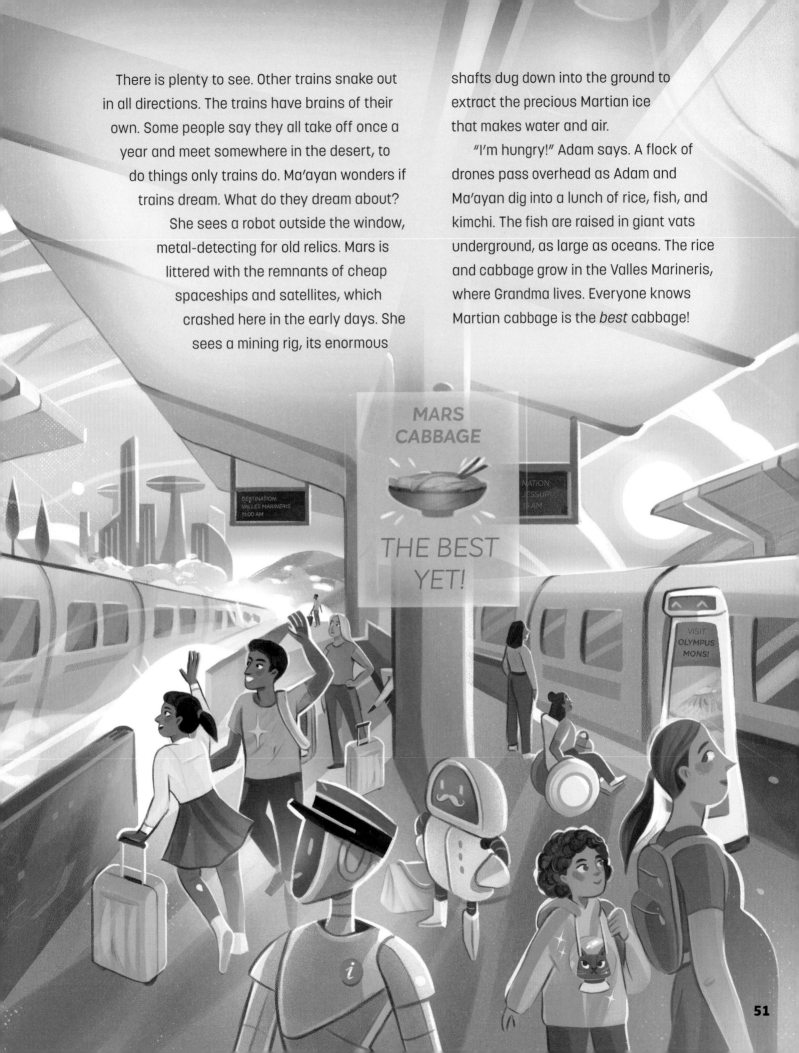

MARS
CABBAGE

THE BEST
YET!

DESTINATION:
VALLES MARINERIS
11:00 AM

NATION:
JESSUP
15 AM

VISIT
OLYMPUS
MONS!

Olympus Mons

Olympus Mons, the tallest mountain in the solar system, is so huge that it juts out of the Martian atmosphere. For comparison, you could fit two and a half Mount Everests into it. Now imagine climbing a mountain this tall all the way to the edge of space!

Domed towns go past: Port Jessup, Yaniv Town, and Enid. The train doesn't stop. It has a long way to go. It zooms across the sands, faster than any train on Earth. Ma'ayan thinks she'd like to visit Earth one day. Then she sees a giant sandstorm coming! The train plunges into the dusty storm and cuts through it. On the other side the sun shines. Soon Ma'ayan sees Olympus Mons. It is the biggest mountain in the whole solar system! People like to try and climb it in spacesuits.

Eat your cabbage

It might sound funny to talk about Martian cabbage, but this leafy vegetable is full of health benefits—and scientists say it can even offer some protection from radiation! Cabbages can also be pickled and preserved for a long time, as with the German sauerkraut or Korean kimchi. These fermented foods are full of good bacteria that helps the human gut—and they taste great, too!

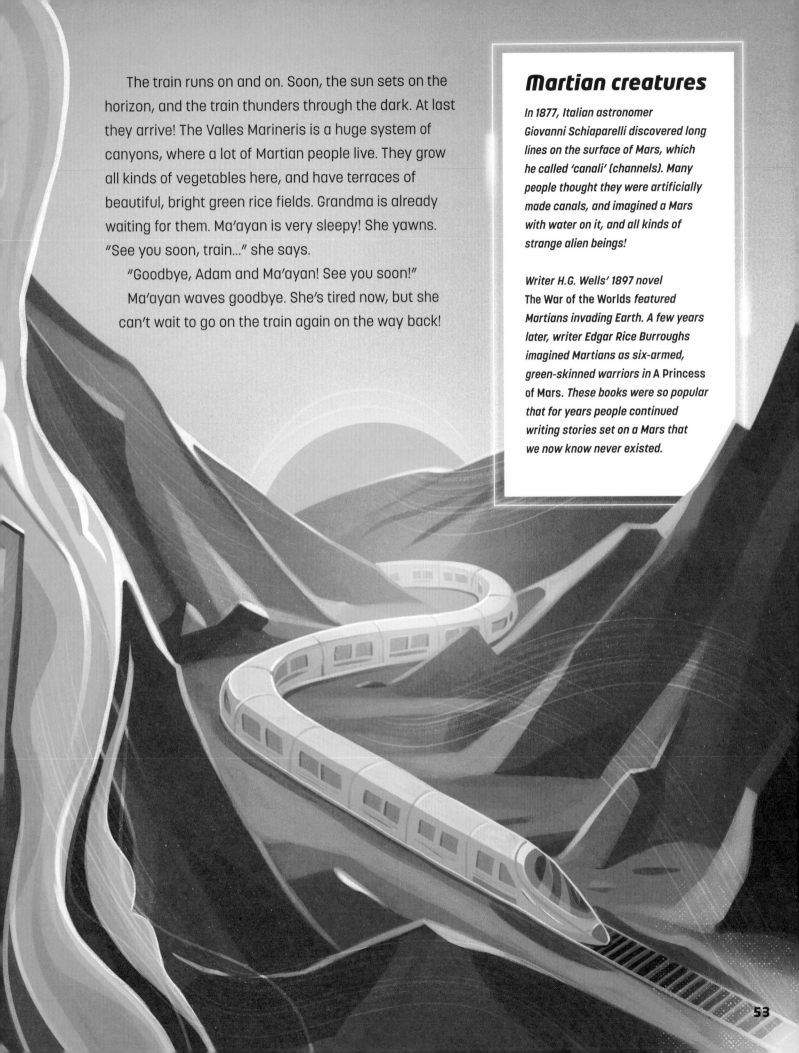

The train runs on and on. Soon, the sun sets on the horizon, and the train thunders through the dark. At last they arrive! The Valles Marineris is a huge system of canyons, where a lot of Martian people live. They grow all kinds of vegetables here, and have terraces of beautiful, bright green rice fields. Grandma is already waiting for them. Ma'ayan is very sleepy! She yawns. "See you soon, train…" she says.

"Goodbye, Adam and Ma'ayan! See you soon!" Ma'ayan waves goodbye. She's tired now, but she can't wait to go on the train again on the way back!

Martian creatures

In 1877, Italian astronomer Giovanni Schiaparelli discovered long lines on the surface of Mars, which he called 'canali' (channels). Many people thought they were artificially made canals, and imagined a Mars with water on it, and all kinds of strange alien beings!

Writer H.G. Wells' 1897 novel The War of the Worlds *featured Martians invading Earth. A few years later, writer Edgar Rice Burroughs imagined Martians as six-armed, green-skinned warriors in* A Princess of Mars. *These books were so popular that for years people continued writing stories set on a Mars that we now know never existed.*

Could there be life on Mars?

Mars isn't a nice place to live. The atmosphere is unbreathable. Surface gravity is low. It is dusty and cold, and its soil is toxic. But the planet does have water in the form of ice. In fact, Mars once had a warm, wet climate similar to Earth.

Orbital
space mirror

Adapting the atmosphere

Terraforming is the idea of transforming an inhospitable planet into something suitable for humans to live on. So how might it work on Mars? First you would need to build up and alter the atmosphere to make it thicker. This would warm up the planet, and stop melted polar ice water from floating off into space.

Heating up

Introducing greenhouse gases could be one way to warm Mars up, as well as introducing plants, or even exploding thermonuclear devices at both of its poles. Another idea would be to use billions of orbital space mirrors to direct more sunlight onto Mars' surface.

Terra-what-now?

Where does the term terraforming come from? The concept has its origins in science fiction, but it was astronomer Carl Sagan who first popularized the idea. Mars is thought of as the most likely candidate for terraforming, but while possible in theory, huge obstacles remain, not least of which the enormous cost and long-term nature of such a huge project.

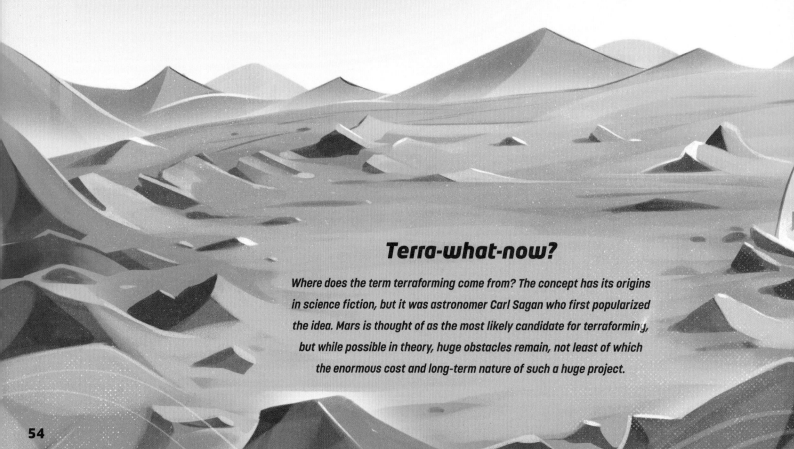

One way ticket

It takes a spaceship about three days to reach the moon from Earth, but the journey to Mars is about seven months! This makes it much more difficult to go—let alone come back. One idea is to send people on a one-way trip. It might sound strange, but when the idea was announced, a lot of people rushed to sign up!

Fact or fiction?

People have always dreamed of Mars, and imagined aliens there. We're still looking for signs of Martian life today! The first spaceship to land on Mars was the *Viking 1* in 1976, and it was followed by many more. Soon there will be a first human to land on Mars!

*A much simpler idea than warming Mars might be to build sealed **biodomes** on the surface, and dig caves and tunnels underneath.*

MINERS OF THE ASTEROIDS

The asteroid belt is huge. Inuk knows this, but it's still amazing every time they go flying through that enormous ring of rocks that circles all the way around the sun!

Living in the Belt is not like living anywhere else. There's no planet or moon, only asteroids. Inuk thinks of his home on Ceres, the largest asteroid. It lies between Mars and Jupiter.

Ceres is beautiful, with the houses dug into the surface and extending out into space. There are always spaceships, too, coming and going.

Right now, though, Inuk and his family are in the Gray Wolf, both a spaceship and their second home.

They're searching the asteroid field for minerals. Some asteroids are so rich they contain gold or platinum. Some are made of ice, too, which is super valuable for space-born humans!

"Did you ever hear the story of Spacebeard the Pirate?" Inuk's sister Asta asks.

"What? No!" Inuk says.

"Shush," Asta says. "He'll hear you!"

"There are no pirates of the asteroids," Inuk says. He wasn't born yesterday.

"No..." Asta says. "But there used to be... and the most terrible of all was Spacebeard the Terrible."

Mine craft

Many companies are lining up to search for resources in space, such as iron, gold, and platinum. But these resources are unlikely to come back to Earth. They will more likely be used to build bases and ships for further space exploration. The most precious resource of all will be water, which can be used to grow food and make fuel and air from oxygen and hydrogen.

Space treasure

Gold is very valuable on Earth, but did you know it comes from outer space? Because gold is an element, it cannot be made from ordinary chemical reactions. So how is it made? The answer is giant explosions—the colliding of massive stars to be precise. Gold and other metals are then blown out into the universe where they mix with space dust, and might, one day, even form new planets.

DID YOU KNOW?

Scientists estimate that the sun contains about 2.5 trillion tons of gold. That's more than enough gold to fill all of the Earth's oceans!

"What did he do?" Inuk whispers.

"Oh, horrible things!" Asta says happily. "But one day he vanished. And they say he left his treasure behind!"

"What sort of treasure?" Inuk asks sceptically.

"No one knows for sure," Asta says. "*I* heard it's a haunted spaceship filled with gold, guarded by pirate ghosts!"

"I don't believe you," Inuk says nervously.

"*I* heard it's a *map*." Inuk's mom floats in. "Buried on a nameless asteroid. If you find it, it leads you to *aliens*!"

"Oh, come on!" Inuk says. "No one's ever met any aliens."

"No one's met them *yet*," Inuk's mom says and smiles.

Inuk's dad appears. "*I* heard it was a ghost!"

"Aargh!" Inuk says. "Dad! Stop it!" Everyone laughs.

Dad goes back to navigating and Mom supervises the cargo bay. Asta does her homework. But Inuk stares out of the window. He watches the rocks floating in space.

Maybe there really is hidden treasure there, he thinks. And if there is, maybe one day he will find it!

What exactly is an asteroid?

Asteroids are rocks that were left behind from the creation of our solar system about 4.6 billion years ago. Most matter was made into the sun and planets (like Earth), but some smaller pieces got left over.

Asteroid belt

Most asteroids in our solar system orbit the sun in a huge ring between Mars and Jupiter. We call this region the asteroid belt. There are millions of asteroids. Some are the size of pebbles, others are as big as cars or houses, and some are giant and stretch for many miles. The biggest asteroid in the belt, Ceres, was thought to be a tiny planet when it was discovered in 1801.

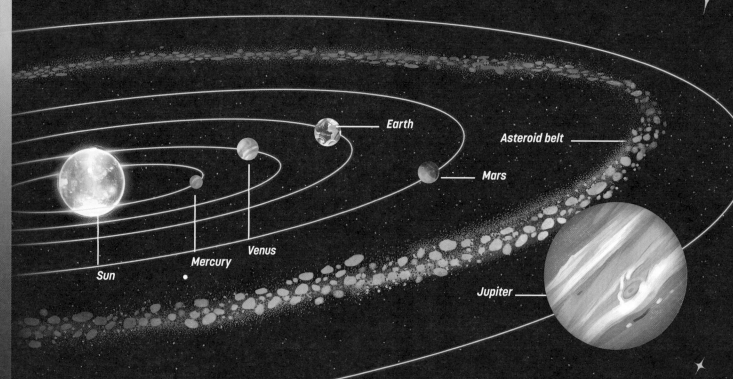

Earth

Asteroid belt

Mars

Venus

Mercury

Sun

Jupiter

Keeping Earth safe

NASA's Center for Near Earth Object Studies asks people to help detect asteroids heading close to Earth—well, within 120 million miles (190 million km), which is close in relation to all of space! Asteroids are defined as anything measuring more than 460 ft (140 m) across. It might not sound like much, but they travel so fast that if they ever hit Earth they would make a big hole. If you have a telescope, why not get involved?

Important asteroids

Asteroids were formed at the same time as all the other objects in the solar system. This means they can give us vital clues about the formation of planets—a little like fossils. Asteroids also contain important things like iron and nickel, which might be needed one day to build space colonies or spaceships!

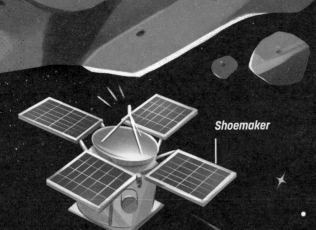

Shoemaker

Observing asteroids

We've been observing asteroids for years, but in 2001, NASA landed a spacecraft called Shoemaker on a near-Earth asteroid called Eros. Then, in 2016, NASA landed on another asteroid, Bennu, and collected samples. These then headed back to Earth to be studied by scientists.

DID YOU KNOW?

If you are ever lucky enough to find a meteorite, you are allowed to keep it!

Meteors and meteorites

Meteors are pieces of asteroids that break off and burn up when they reach Earth's atmosphere. When lots of meteors enter the atmosphere it's called a meteor shower. Meteorites are the pieces that make it to Earth. While rare, it does happen. Some people go hunting for meteorites! They're easiest to find in the desert, but they can be found anywhere—one landed in a garden in the UK in 2021. It was named the Winchcombe meteorite and was billions of years old.

Part 4:
THE FAR FUTURE

What will life be like in 500 years, or even *5,000* years? Will humans have mastered space travel and visited the farthest reaches of the universe? Maybe we'll have adapted our entire solar system into one giant world, or made contact with aliens. Let your imagination run wild, and then discover the science behind how these space adventures could happen one day!

TITAN BY PLANE

Eliot waits inside the huge hangar of the Polyport Airfield. He is going for a flight with Grandpa Ramy! Grandpa Ramy is a pilot.

The plane is similar to the ones on faraway Earth, but it's also a bit like the submarines on Earth. It has an atomic engine, a body made of light acrylic glass, and its own oxygen generator. It's a tiny world within a world!

Eliot straps into the seat. Grandpa takes the stick and the plane glides out of the airlock and into the atmosphere of Titan. It gathers speed and rises into the thick soup of nitrogen and methane. Eliot stares out of the window as Polyphemus Port gets smaller below them. The city is covered in a transparent dome, and the inside is lush with tropical vegetation.

Lord of the Rings of Saturn

Some places on Titan are named after the Lord of the Rings books by J.R.R. Tolkien! There is a place on Titan called Mount Doom, like the volcano, a hill named Bilbo, like the hobbit, and another named Gandalf, after the famous fictional wizard.

"Where are we going?" Eliot asks Grandpa.

"To the beach!" Grandpa says. He loves to fly. He flies all over Titan, Saturn's largest moon.

Eliot sees other planes, as well as hot-air balloons. Titan is perfect for flying!

"Look!" Grandpa says. "It's raining again!"

Eliot watches the clouds and the methane rain. The land passes slowly below. They fly over mountains, rivers, and small towns and villages in domes, or dug underground. Eliot also sees little robots, cars with people in them, and mining rigs that extract power from the valuable methane. He loves flying with Grandpa—even when a storm is brewing!

Soon, the little plane tilts as it begins to descend. Now Eliot sees it—the Kraken Mare, Titan's great sea. Then the island of Mayda Insula comes into view.

Grandpa Ramy eases the plane down for landing. Eliot helps him offload the cargo—everything from watermelons from Polyphemus Port to packages from Earth and Mars. Titan pilots go everywhere!

Eliot already knows he wants to be a pilot when he grows up—just like Grandpa Ramy.

Going to the beach

The biggest sea on Titan is called the Kraken Mare, named after the mythical sea monster! There is a large island on the sea called the Mayda Insula—it was the first island not on Earth to ever be named.

Cassini *explored Saturn for 13 years*

Cassini

Titan's surface had always been something of a mystery due to its thick clouds, but in 2004 the spacecraft Cassini orbited Saturn and landed a probe on the surface of Titan a year later. This revealed a rather fascinating environment!

Fly me to the moons... of Saturn

Titan is the second largest moon in the solar system. It is so large that it was originally thought to be a planet! It orbits the gas giant Saturn, in the far reaches of our solar system.

Atmosphere made of nitrogen and methane

Magnificent moon

Although it's so far, humans have been visiting Titan for many years—first with telescopes and more recently with space probes. *Pioneer 11* was the first human-made object to encounter Titan in 1979, and we've been exploring it with robotic probes ever since. But why Titan? According to NASA, it could be one of the best places in space for humans to live, as it contains all the building blocks for life. In fact, in some ways Titan resembles Earth billions of years ago.

Thick clouds

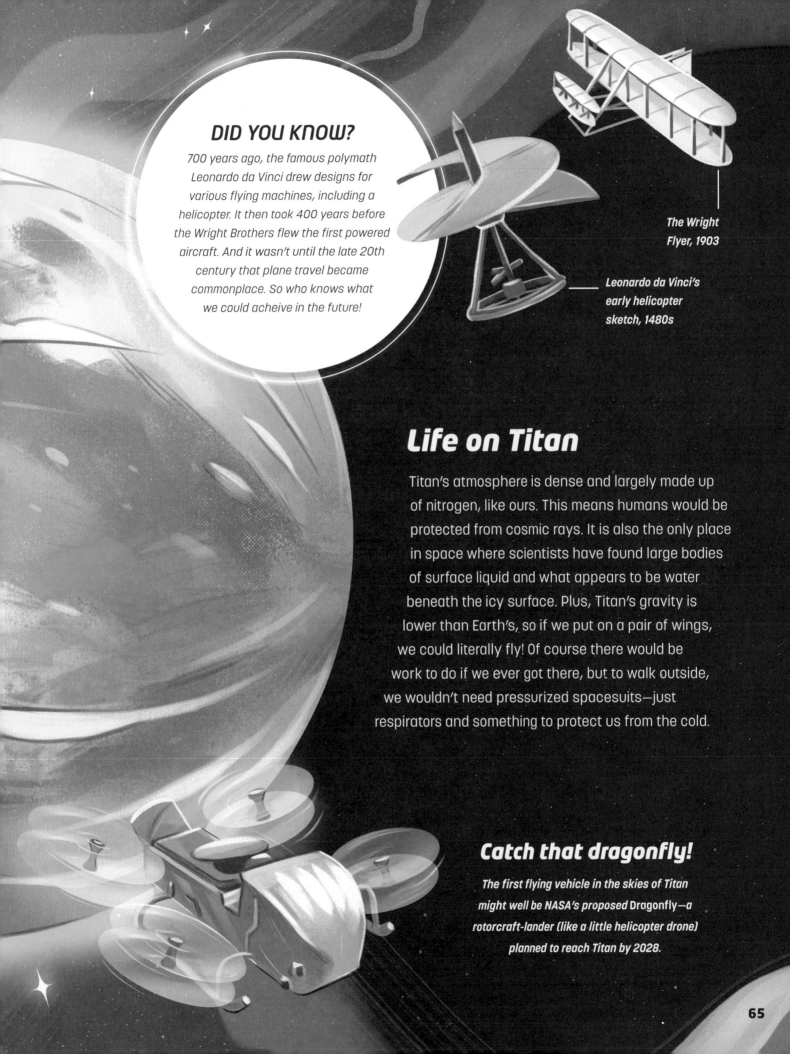

The Wright Flyer, 1903

Leonardo da Vinci's early helicopter sketch, 1480s

Life on Titan

Titan's atmosphere is dense and largely made up of nitrogen, like ours. This means humans would be protected from cosmic rays. It is also the only place in space where scientists have found large bodies of surface liquid and what appears to be water beneath the icy surface. Plus, Titan's gravity is lower than Earth's, so if we put on a pair of wings, we could literally fly! Of course there would be work to do if we ever got there, but to walk outside, we wouldn't need pressurized spacesuits—just respirators and something to protect us from the cold.

Catch that dragonfly!

The first flying vehicle in the skies of Titan might well be NASA's proposed Dragonfly—a rotorcraft-lander (like a little helicopter drone) planned to reach Titan by 2028.

STARSHIP TO TAU CETI

"Many years ago, long before you were born, children, *The Sunflower* was built in the great space docks around Mars," the teacher says.

The teacher continues, "It slingshot around the sun and headed out of the solar system into galactic space. We were one of the first starships to leave our home!"

Aurora doesn't agree. The ship *is* her home! She was born here, and it is a whole world, no different from this 'Earth' the teacher talks about. *The Sunflower* has everything—gardens, movie theaters, playgrounds, and parks. It rains once a week, from the overhead sprinklers. *The Sunflower* is awesome. What did Aurora need Earth for?

"Don't forget we're going to the zoo next week," the teacher says as class finishes. "Bring plenty of water!"

On Earth they had all the water they could want, but water is precious on *The Sunflower*. Every drop has to be recycled.

Don't try this at home!

Cryonics is an idea where people are placed on pause using extremely low temperatures so that they can be 'woken up' in the future, perhaps when they arrive at a distant planet. Some people are already trying to do this—the first person to be cryogenically frozen was all the way back in 1967. Whatever you do, though, don't try this at home!

Aurora's father is a water engineer, so she knows all about it! After school, she and Yukimi visit the control center, where Aurora's mother is serving as that year's Captain. A captain is elected every year to manage the ship. It's a big job, though, and Aurora's mother doesn't have as much time to play with her as she used to, which makes Aurora sad.

On their way to the control center, they stop at the hydroponic gardens where all the food is grown. They wave to Yukimi's dad—he's a gardener. He is tending to the beautiful flowers that grow on the ship. He gives them a sunflower!

They also pass the cryogenics chambers, which are strictly off limits. These are where some passengers from Old Earth are frozen, waiting to be woken up when they reach their destination! The ship is traveling to a star called Tau Ceti, which is 12 light-years from Earth. Though the ship travels very fast, space is huge, so the journey will take generations. Aurora doesn't care about getting there. She loves the journey itself!

When they reach the control center everyone is busy. On the screens, Aurora can see space and their destination. It's so far away! But she's in no hurry. She loves her home on *The Sunflower.*

Welcome to the neighborhood!

Some of Earth's nearby stars include Barnard's Star, Wolf 359, and Tau Ceti. We now know many of these stars have planets around them. Tau Ceti has seven planets that we know of, two of which could potentially be similar enough to Earth to contain life. We don't know for sure yet—but wouldn't it be great to find out?

We are here

Are we there yet?

A famous astronomer named Carl Sagan once said that "there are more stars in our universe than there are grains of sand on all the beaches on Earth."

The Milky Way

If you look up at night, you might be able to see the Milky Way—our home galaxy. It's a nebula galaxy with four spiral 'arms' swirling around a huge black hole in the center. We live in the Orion Arm, far away from the center—sort of like the distant suburbs of the galaxy. To give an idea of how big it is, imagine that the Milky Way was the size of a continent. Our solar system would be about the size of a tiny coin in comparison. Our own 'galactic neighborhood' includes stars and planets only a few light-years away. Though relatively close on a galactic scale, that's still really, really far!

Far space

So, how might we get to these stars one day? Existing technologies are too slow. Even the nearest planetary system to our own, Alpha Centauri, would take a century to reach with current technology. But humans have been thinking about this problem for a long time, and scientists are working on new ideas, which include tiny robotic probes that could make the journey to our galactic neighbors in the near future.

To boldly go

Instead of going to space in person, some people think it may one day be possible to upload a person's mind into a device to live forever, or to travel deep into the universe. Perhaps future space exploration won't be done by humans. Maybe astronauts will be sentient robots or AI systems?

Faraway travel

Solar sail

One idea is to use the power of the sun to accelerate tiny robots into space. Like boats on the sea, these would use huge sails to catch the solar wind (radiation pressure).

Slingshot

Another idea is to 'slingshot' a ship around the sun, a little like spinning a ball really fast before letting it go.

Bussard Ramjet

In 1960, scientist Robert Bussard, had an idea for a big ship that would catch hydrogen from space to power it.

Generation starships

Perhaps we will build ships that travel slowly, carrying people for generations. Only the original passengers' great-great-great grandchildren would reach the stars!

FIRST ENCOUNTERS

"What's that?" Yukimi asks.

There is a light blinking on the communication panel in the control center of *The Sunflower*. Aurora's mother frowns.

"It must be a mistake with the system. That's all."

"But what is it?" Aurora asks, now interested too.

Her mother laughs. "It's for getting signals from outside the ship," she says.

"But there is nothing outside the ship," Aurora says.

"Exactly," her mother says.

"Unless..." Yukimi says.

"Unless what?" Aurora asks.

"Unless there is," Yukimi says.

"But there can't be!" Aurora says. "Can there?"

"Let's see what it says," Aurora's mother says. "Maybe it's some noise." She presses buttons. It does sound like noise at first. It's just beeps. It goes:

Beep... Beep beep... Beep beep beep...

And then repeats after a while.

"Wait. That's not noise!" Yukimi says. "It's a number sequence!"

"But..." Aurora's mom says. She starts pressing buttons furiously. Everyone in the control room turns to look. Soon they're all busy at their stations. Then—

"There!"

But what do they look like?

No one knows what aliens will look like. Right now, scientists are searching for evidence of life on Mars. Scientists also think we should be looking for Earthlike planets, with liquid water and plenty of air. Think how strange some of the creatures on Earth are. TV shows often feature aliens who look like us, but what if aliens look more like spiders, or jellyfish, or kangaroos? Or maybe they won't look like anything we can imagine!

On the big screen in front of them they can see space. There, in the far distance, is the destination star. Somewhere far behind is Earth and its sun. Out here there is just the darkness of galactic space. And for a moment Aurora can't see anything, but then—

"There!" Yukimi says, pointing.

It looks like a tiny pebble. The telescopes focus on it, and gradually it becomes bigger on the screen. It still just looks like a rock, maybe an asteroid floating in space. It couldn't be a spaceship. Could it?

"Try to reply to it," Yukimi says. She's practically jumping up and down in exhilaration.

"What should I say?" Aurora's mother asks.

"Let me think... Try prime numbers!" Yukimi says. Yukimi loves numbers. Aurora's mother sends a signal to the alien rock. The beeps translate to 2...3...5...7...11...

Nothing happens for a long time. But then the comms come to life with a new series of beeps!

"It says..." Yukimi concentrates. "13! 17! 19!"

"What does that mean?" Aurora asks.

"It means they understand prime numbers! Whoever they are—they're intelligent! It's their way of saying hello!" Yukimi says.

"But who are they?" Aurora's mom asks. "There are no human ships here other than us."

"It's because they're not human," Yukimi says. "They must be aliens!"

They stare at the screen. The little alien rock floats in space. It could be a hollowed-out asteroid, Yukimi thinks. She wonders what the aliens inside look like. She's excited to talk to them some more. She knows they will become best friends!

ET, call us!

Famous science fiction writer Arthur C. Clarke once said there's only one question that matters—are we alone in the universe? He said that both answers, Yes or No, are terrifying. If we are alone in the vastness of space, then *Yikes!* If we are not alone, then—*Yikes!!!*

Is anyone out there?

Named after astrophysicist, Frank Drake, the Drake equation estimates how many intelligent alien civilizations might exist in our galaxy, the Milky Way. It says there could be as many as 182 million, and depends on the rate of star formation, the percentage of stars that have planets, and the number that might create intelligent life. Also, the number that broadcast their existence with signals we can detect. There should be a lot of aliens out there! So why can't we see them?

Our own planet

So far, our own species has found no evidence of alien life in space, let alone intelligent life. This may one day change. In the meantime, this means we are hugely special and unique—as individuals and as a species. It also means our tiny blue planet is special and unique. Maybe it's important that we venture out into the distant reaches of space. But it's even more important that we take care of what we have right here, right now, in our own backyards and beyond!

A message from afar

What would happen if we did receive a message from outer space? The answer would probably depend on the nature of the message, or whether its senders planned to come to Earth. People might be very excited or very scared. Either way, it would be an incredible event. And hopefully humanity would come together and understand that what unites us is stronger than whatever divides us.

Why haven't they come?

Italian scientist Enrico Fermi came up with a simple idea called the Fermi Paradox. The huge size of the universe surely means other intelligent life forms exist. But there has never been any evidence of them. So where are they? One answer is that maybe we're looking for the wrong thing. Or we're looking in the wrong places. Perhaps aliens are really rare. No one knows for sure. But we keep looking!

WOW!

In 1977, a radio telescope called Big Ear detected something strange—a powerful signal from the Sagittarius constellation! A few days later, scientist, Jerry Ehman was looking at the data and noticed the signal. He circled it and wrote "Wow!" next to it. The signal never repeated. It is still considered the strongest candidate for an alien message ever received.

LIFE ON A DYSON SPHERE

The teacher's voice whispers in Luna's mind, but she is bored. Today they're studying 21st century Earth. Boring! Earth doesn't even exist anymore. Instead, there is just the World—and it is all around Luna.

The classroom floats in space around the sun, a transparent bubble of indestructible material. From her pod desk, Luna can see out in all directions. A long, long time ago, engineers began dragging all the planets of the solar system into orbit around the sun. Then they took them apart, to build billions and billions of habitats and satellites. They orbit the sun from the same distance as the old, vanished Earth once did.

There are worldlets, which are small worlds, with oceans and forests, and others with huge machines that harvest power directly from the sun. Giant ships go to other solar systems in the universe, to visit some of the worlds humanity has built.

Space is big and full of marvels! So why does Luna have to learn about tiny Earth and the people who lived on it such a long time ago?

DID YOU KNOW?

There are no clouds in space. This is why collecting solar energy from the sun—or another star—is highly efficient compared to doing it back on Earth.

Goldilocks zone

The distance from Earth to the sun is perfect for us humans. We call that distance one Astronomical Unit (or 1 AU). That's approximately 93 million miles (150 million km)! When we search for alien life, we look for planets in the so-called 'Goldilocks zone.' Those planets are just the right distance from their star to have liquid water. Like Goldilocks in the story, they are not too hot, and not too cold—they're just right!

Luna's friend Artemis sends her a telepathic message. *Let's get out of here!* she says. The two girls sneak out of class. The classroom is connected to their own personal worldlet by a long curving bridge. There is no roof, but an invisible force field keeps the atmosphere in.

"I wish I lived on old Earth," Artemis says wistfully. "It must have been amazing! Imagine—a whole world to run around in!"

"But we have lots and lots of worlds!" Luna says. "And besides, people in the 21st century were like..." She tries to think. She didn't pay much attention in class.

"They lived in, like, caves," she finishes.

"I'd love to visit a real cave!" Artemis says. "I wish we kept Earth as it was. Then I could visit it, not just in the simulation."

"But the simulation is super real!" The teacher made them visit old Earth once. It was noisy, dirty, and full of people!

"I'm going to be a historian when I grow up," Artemis says, "so I can learn about the people who came before us."

"I'm going to be a starship captain, so I can visit other worlds—but we'll always be friends, won't we?" Luna asks anxiously.

Artemis laughs and pulls her friend along as they reach their beautiful home-world. "Of course we will!" she says.

The Kardashev Scale

Russian astronomer Nikolai Kardashev created the Kardashev Scale in 1964. The scale measures the technological advancement of civilizations by looking at how much energy they have access to. So, one way to detect aliens might be to look for energy harvesting structures in deep space. Currently on Earth we only collect a tiny amount of energy from our nearest star, the sun. But building huge structures that encircle stars would allow us to collect much greater amounts of solar energy—even all the energy a star produces!

Level I Civilization

Planetary level of energy consumption— like our contemporary Earth.

Level II Civilization

Capable of using the energy from an entire star—by using a Dyson Sphere, for example.

Level III Civilization

Can use the power of an entire galaxy.

Level IV Civilization

Kadashev thought no civilization could get more powerful than III, so he never suggested IV. But some people took the idea even farther and suggested type IV could harness the power of an entire universe!

A Dyson what?

Imagine a world as large as an entire star. Although it's hypothetical, a Dyson sphere could achieve this one day. It may even be necessary in order to provide energy for our ever growing population!

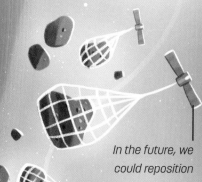

In the future, we could reposition asteroids

Freeman Dyson

The Dyson Sphere is named after a physicist and mathematician called Freeman Dyson. In 1960, he said that any super advanced civilization would need to build megastructures in space to harvest the huge amounts of energy they'd need.

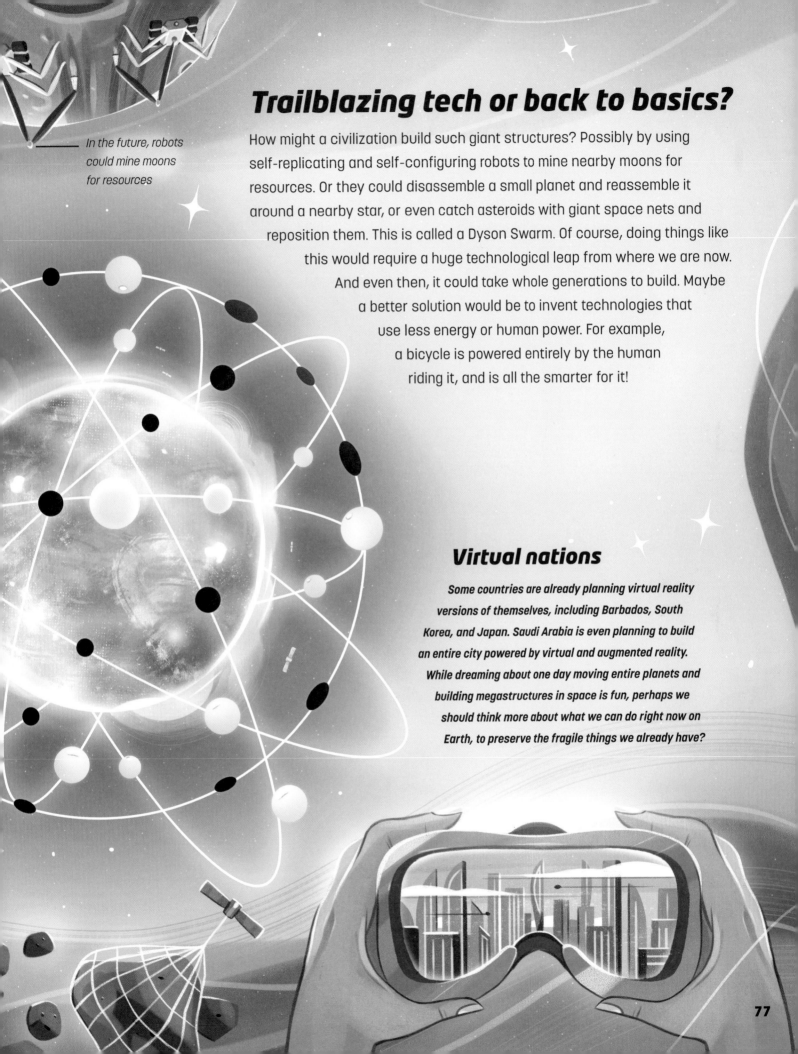

Trailblazing tech or back to basics?

In the future, robots could mine moons for resources

How might a civilization build such giant structures? Possibly by using self-replicating and self-configuring robots to mine nearby moons for resources. Or they could disassemble a small planet and reassemble it around a nearby star, or even catch asteroids with giant space nets and reposition them. This is called a Dyson Swarm. Of course, doing things like this would require a huge technological leap from where we are now. And even then, it could take whole generations to build. Maybe a better solution would be to invent technologies that use less energy or human power. For example, a bicycle is powered entirely by the human riding it, and is all the smarter for it!

Virtual nations

Some countries are already planning virtual reality versions of themselves, including Barbados, South Korea, and Japan. Saudi Arabia is even planning to build an entire city powered by virtual and augmented reality. While dreaming about one day moving entire planets and building megastructures in space is fun, perhaps we should think more about what we can do right now on Earth, to preserve the fragile things we already have?

AFTERWORD

More than half a century ago, a student sprayed graffiti on the wall of the Sorbonne University in Paris. It said "The future will only contain whatever we put in to it now". Quite correct. Whatever our history, whatever our present, our futures remain unwritten. But our futures are created by what you, then others, decide to do today and everyday thereafter.

But that's not all. The future is not a singular destination. It is not somewhere that we all arrive at once. Similarly, it is not somewhere that remains fixed or unchanging. The future is always being built and can always be changed.

So, if you want to build space rockets, grow vegetables in underwater cities, collect space junk, or simply plant a few trees here on Earth, nothing is stopping you. Never let anyone tell you otherwise. Everything is possible until it's not. The future belongs to you.

Be curious about it. Influence it. Make it awesome!

—Lavie and Richard

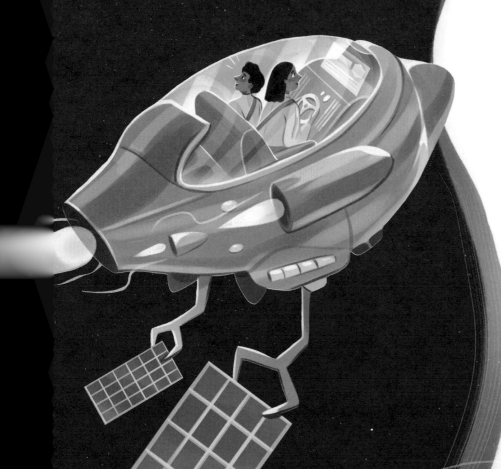

GLOSSARY

Anesthesiologist

A specialist doctor who gives medication to patients that prevents pain during surgery and other procedures

Apollo 11

The American space mission that first landed humans on the moon

Apollo 17

The eleventh and final Apollo mission, and the sixth and most recent time humans have set foot on the moon

Artificial Intelligence (AI)

The ability of a computer or machine to think and learn like a human

Asteroid

A chunk of rock or very small planet that usually travel around the sun

Autonomous

Controls itself and is not led by anything or anyone else

Biodiversity

The variety of plants and animals that live in an area

Black hole

Area in space where gravity is so strong that nothing can escape it, including light

Carbon dioxide

A gas that is produced by animals, people, and chemical reactions, and is absorbed by plants. Too much is bad for life on Earth

Comet

An object made of dust, ice, and frozen gases that were left over from the formation of the solar system. It orbits the sun, and, when close to it, it develops a tail made of gas

Compost

A mixture that contains mostly decayed organic matter. It is used to help plants grow

Constellation

A group of stars that forms a pattern

Cosmic rays

High-energy particles from outer space that travel at nearly the speed of light

Drone

A flying machine with no pilot

Gaia

Ancient Greek goddess of Earth. The Gaia theory suggests everything on Earth is one single living system

Gas giant

A large planet mainly made of gas

Geneticist

Someone who studies genetics, including how genes vary and how they are inherited

Glider

A light aircraft that flies without an engine

Heavier-than-air

Relates to an aircraft that flies despite being more dense than air

Helium

A light, colorless, and odorless gas

Humanoid

Resembling a human

Hydroponics

A method of growing plants without soil

Infrared

A type of energy that is invisible to humans

Internet of Everything

A network that links people, data, processes, and things

Internet of Things

A network of devices that connect and exchange data

Light-year

The distance light travels in one year

Megacity

A very large city, typically with a population of more than 10 million

Meteoroid

A small object that orbits the sun and becomes a meteor if it enters Earth's atmosphere

Nutrients

Food or other substances that animals and plants need to survive

Orbit

A regular, repeating path that one object takes around another, such as the Earth around the sun

Pollution

Harmful substances in the air, soil, or water

Pressurized

Sealed to maintain the air pressure that humans need to survive

Propulsion system

A machine that produces force to move objects

Raw material

An unused material taken from nature without being processed

Revival

The process of something becoming popular or active again

Tanker

A vehicle or vessel built to carry liquid or gas

INDEX

ACKNOWLEDGMENTS

Lavie: For Eliot

Richard: This book is dedicated to all of the children around the world who believe in fantastic futures. It is also dedicated to those joyful parents and courageous teachers that are not imprisoned by other people's thinking and believe in the power of children's minds, especially their curiosity and imagination, to transform life on Earth and far beyond.